Quail
In My Bed

By Burley Packwood

QUAIL IN MY BED

Published by
Quantum Press of Arizona
17823 99th Drive
Sun City, AZ 85373

ISBN 0-9624358-0-5
Library of Congress Catalog Card Number: 89-092060

Printed in the United States of America

Second printing 1992

To Betsi,
My wife, my love and my inspiration
and, of course, Pedra.

Tom Wolfe

With special thanks to Jerry Cline for his extreme patience and for sharing his word processing knowledge, technical assistance and layout of this book. Without him my manuscript would still be in a tangle.

God was kind to me the day Mary Westheimer answered my call for help.
I shall be eternally grateful for her advice and stimulating encouragement. Thank you Mary and You too, up there.

My long time friend, Tom Wolfe, provided the full page sketches of Pedra. I missed him when he lived among the Athabascan Indians and welcomed him back when he mushed 2800 miles by dog sled from the Yukon to our mutual home in Montana. He is an acknowledged artist and expert big game outfitter and guide.

Chapter One

My wife either owns the sharpest eyes in Sun City, Arizona, or her discovery was an act of God. Considering her bifocals, the Dicty may have played a greater role.

I remember sliding open the patio door that brilliant July morning because the back doorbell had been insistent. Quickly crossing our tiny herb garden and side stepping powerfully pungent rosemary and basil plants, I unlatched the gate.

"I've got a quail!" I heard Betsi shriek through thick white walls. "Look! I've got a baby Gambel's quail." She laughed excitedly and held aloft a blob of flesh and fuzz and—as the gate swung ajar—thrust it into my face. I inspected the walnut-sized, ugly chick without comment, for the dilemma of adopting a dying quail while preparing for a two-month camping trip tempered my enthusiasm.

"Isn't it beautiful?" Motherly love sparkled in Betsi's blue eyes, but her genius for overstatement left me breathless. "It's nearly dead." She quickly advised, "Let's take it out of the heat." Blistering sun caught her forehead and she flushed crimson from desert fire and maternal enthusiasm.

Death is not beautiful and the disgracefully homely chick draped limply across her protective hand. Its feeble head sank loosely between her fingers and thready, irregular heartbeats pulsed quite visibly through matted fuzz. To me, dehydration and heat stroke had clearly claimed another victim. Its closed eyes and open mouth suggested a shrunken plucked duck like those which hang in Chinese markets. Then suddenly its mouth stretched wide open in an exaggerated yawn, hesitated as though to speak, but drifted quietly closed. No sound flowed from the chick and it apparently stopped breathing, seemingly dead.

Astounded—and secretly gratified at its demise—I smiled inwardly and finally said, "It's dead. Don't bring it inside."

Ignoring my protests, Betsi touched my arm in a gesture of urgency. "Quick! In the house!" She sped across the small garden and into the air-conditioned patio, hastily explaining how she had gone for her morning bicycle ride and nearly had run over what she believed to be a poinsettia leaf on the sizzling alley asphalt. Instinct guided her. She spun around and examined the suspected leaf again. A newly-hatched Gamble's quail, barely larger than her thumbnail, stretched dehydrating in 110 degree sun. She couldn't believe her luck, tucked the baby inside her bosom and quickly wheeled home to share our good fortune.

My mind, cramped by more than sixty-five years of life without quail children, did not instantly accept our good luck for we had no plans for quail adoption. Quite the contrary. We had scheduled, beginning at sunrise next day, a drive toward Canada in our VW bus, camping on the San Juan islands and, pivoting south, drifting leisurely down the California coastline. The long-planned retirement trip positively contained no provision for quail passengers. Calamity, in many guises, had befallen us previously, but under present circumstances I could not have been more prejudiced against quail adoption than if Betsi had driven a flock of ostriches through the living room.

Seemingly mesmerized, she spoke continuously to the chick in low, soothing tones as though to a cribbed infant. "We've been waiting a long time for a little bird like you," she told the dying quail.

I searched, quickly and systematically, for clues to support her amazing statement. Never, by word or suggestion, had I encouraged her to believe that I (or we) ever wanted a baby quail. We cherished and admired the graceful birds along boulevards, but adoption, training, responsibility? Never! Especially today. Reviewing the mountainous disorganized piles of camping gear around us I shuddered. With luck—and without quail—a sunrise departure seemed barely possible. "No!" I told myself again. "We've never, never wanted a quail."

Betsi, dreaming in other worlds, suddenly awakened from her trance. "What shall we feed the baby?"

"Arsenic," I told her quietly, but she pretended not to hear.

2

"I'll call Millie. Millie knows. She knows everything." She cuddled the chick against her cheek and dialed her friend, a known bird lover.

Moments later she replaced the receiver. "I told you we'd have no problem. The formula is a small can of dog food and canned spinach mixed with crumbled soda crackers, a hard-cooked egg and dried milk. That's it." She gazed lovingly at the ugly infant and stroked its head with her thumb. "The formula is balanced," she told me as though it was a statement that would ultimately wind up in *Great Discoveries of Science*.

"Be sensible," I pleaded. "We don't need a quail. We don't want a quail. We can't take a quail camping. In God's name, listen to reason!" My voice rose to a dangerous level but Betsi did not notice.

Common sense seldom charted her course and she clucked at the infant. "We'll need applesauce too, just a smidgen to clear its craw. Too much will cause diarrhea."

Her vanished susceptibility to logic defeated me and I threw my hands up in despair. "God help us," I thought as she dribbled three whiskey drops into a jigger of warm water and offered the baby a tot of Jim Beam.

By early afternoon, the quail still lived. It lay comatose on a soft cotton bed breathing with great difficulty. Every breath appeared to be its last, but as day drifted into twilight, its delicate life thread, stretched dangerously thin, seemed a little stronger as we tackled the small mountain of canned food and camping supplies.

Thoughts of travel with an infant invalid bird nagged me and I finally cried out in desperation: "Our life would be simpler if that damned bird died."

Betsi whipped around, her voice hoarse with determination. "Don't ever talk that way. This chick will live," she shouted. I retreated in surprise. Vague uneasiness overcame me as I recalled other nursing victories with a crippled mockingbird and a malodorous and unfriendly porcupine. Both survived. When Betsi decided to nurse a cripple, she defied death. Now her drumbeat of determination rang through the house and cold sweat dripped down my back.

Suddenly she leaped up, whirled as if snake-bitten and—all thoughts of travel preparation forgotten—shouted, "We need a cage for our baby."

4

"We need a casket," I thought. "The chick can't raise its head much less fly away."

But her mind flew to problems of restraint. Masterbuilder Betsi could build nearly anything and now she initiated mental construction of the cage. "I'll build it with quarter-inch mesh wire," she said. "It'll collapse and can be stored under our camper bed." Tidying her hair, she grasped a purse and raced through the kitchen to the garage but returned almost instantly. Picking up the chick from its cotton cradle, she thrust the fragile quail into my hands, then paused at the kitchen door. "Don't let Pedro die while I'm gone," she warned.

"Pedro?"

"Yes. That's his name. Pete." And she was gone.

I contemplated the bird in my hand and realized I held the chance of a lifetime. The fate of a congenial camping trip hung in the balance and I was not inclined to allow a dying quail to interfere with it. Only fragments of life remained. Three suffocating seconds would shuffle Pedro through death's door without a trace on my conscience. Of course I'd have to face Betsi but ninety per cent of all infant quail die early and odds had been against Pedro's survival since his masquerade as a poinsettia leaf. The decision rested in my hand and I closed my fist around the bird.

Instinctively the frail chick stretched a pink leg against my palm and a tiny toe, so frail and delicate I marvelled at its construction, reached and found my little finger. Helplessly the feeble foot grasped and barely squeezed. My fist relaxed. Then a strange thing happened. A defeated eye opened in an apparent wink of thanks, its mouth slowly spread wide and I fed him whiskied water. He managed another drizzle before Betsi bounced home thirty minutes later. She inspected Pedro and tickled a huge multicolored feather duster in my face. "Pedro's security blanket," she grinned. "He'll need this in the mountains."

She dropped a roll of wire mesh strong enough to imprison an eagle on the floor and quickly cut and hinged four pieces into a neat collapsible package. "We'll seal the top with mosquito netting and spring clothespins," she told me. Turning to Pedro, she smiled triumphantly. "That'll hold you." Pedro did not hear and sank into a deeper slumber.

The wee sleeping puffball breathed slowly and deeply, each breath a challenge, throughout the afternoon. A goose-necked incandescent lamp above maintained his body heat, but it seemed impossible he could survive each succeeding hour much less a camping trip. I was encouraged.

The blast-furnace day dragged to a close and intimidating piles of clothing, food and equipment rounded into organized stacks. Roach motels guarded the outside entrances and I double locked all windows. We were finally ready for loading.

Summer hunger overcame us and we nibbled tomato and avocado salad while chaperoning Pedro under the incubator lamp. Without explaining, Betsi pushed her chair from the table. "We've forgotten the formula."

"Formula?"

"Pedro's food. He has to eat, too." She arose from the table and, after observing my frustration made a face. "Oh don't be such an old poop. Pedro won't eat much and he won't be any trouble."

My grumbling continued as we entered the busy supermarket.

A familiar sound greeted us at the door. Above the low, efficient whine of the huge air conditioner rose an insistent peep. Betsi and I exchanged glances. "There's a baby quail in here," she whispered. "Another baby!"

Peering down the neat rows of merchandise, she homed in on the penetrating cheep. It erupted on the floor around the vegetable department. During a brief lull in the persistent cheeping a tiny gray phantom streaked across the slippery tile and buzzed under an artichoke display. There it rested, peeping loudly. Without hesitation Betsi dropped to her knees, bent under the counter, and snatched the chick into her brassiere. "Let's go", she whispered. The quailnapping happened so swiftly I had no time to argue.

"What about Pedro's formula?"

"Formula? Oh, that's what we came for. You get it. Check the list and don't forget applesauce."

We approached the checkout stand with canned spinach, dog food and one hollering infant quail in Betsi's bosom. Outside the market I asked, "Don't you feel like a shoplifter?"

"I feel more like a mother," she said as vast quantities of common sense spilled onto the parking lot.

A sinking sense of despair overcame me and I experienced the feeling of losing a battle without knowing which basic tactic had been violated. My reserves—if ever I owned any—were vanishing into vapors of maternal emotion. Silence claimed me for a while and, slowly digesting my dilemma, I breathed deeply, gathering energy. "What in hell are we going to do with TWO quail?"

Betsi smiled. "We'll find a way." She pulled her blouse open and peeked at the squalling chick snuggling in her brassiere. "Hello, little girl. Welcome aboard, Pedra."

The sun disappeared and the sky blazed with brush-fire splendor. I flicked on driving lights and color intensified for we seemed enveloped in a psychedelic kaleidoscope. I blinked several times rapidly for orientation. Reality had vanished. In a millennium I could not conceive camping five-thousand miles with two toddling quail.

I felt alone. Abandoned by a stubborn wife and the possibility of two squawking infants sharing my camp bed detonated a series of stomach cramps in my gut. Peace and serenity of retirement—those golden years so incessantly dramatized by poets and films—oozed from me and I placed a hand on my aching stomach and traced fingers downward. Pain radiated from my groin and I probed tentatively: a hernia? I didn't know what to do. A cloud of misery and self-pity enveloped me and I wailed, "Why now?"

Betsi patted my knee. "It's like family planning. If they come, they come. You don't always pick the time."

My patience cracked and desperately I shouted, "We are not camping with those quail! Never! Do you hear me?"

Betsi looked up in surprise. "You can't be serious. They've adopted us."

I didn't hesitate. "I've never been more serious. Call Millie the instant we get home and ask her if she'll take them. They are not going with us and that's final."

To keep peace with my partner I searched every direction for an excuse to keep the babies, but found not a single one. I closed my eyes briefly and recalled a tactic used successfully—although not frequently—in other hours of despair. When decisions lay in the balance, I simply out shouted her and determined to do so now. Beginning calmly, I detailed logical reasons for not embracing quail travel, my voice and tempo rising in the darkened car. Finally, in a burst of determination my lips bared in an actual snarl and I shouted violently into her ear, "We're not taking those birds. Understand?" Completely spent, I quietly reflected my hollow victory, for Betsi did not reply. She sat silently—in what I perceived to be quiet surrender—stroking Pedra's head. "I love you, little girl," she said.

Darkness pressed across the desert into the White Tank Mountains and we drove to our garden condominium in silence. I reviewed the day that had begun so promising and ended so disastrously with only minor satisfaction for—and I smiled inwardly—at least the quail were not going as long as I made decisions in our home. ➤

Chapter Two

When the red VW camper staggered from the garage next morning at sunrise, two day-old quail nagged non-stop at my elbow. I had been adamant, but Betsi had not listened. She had bundled both birds into a stout cardboard apple box carpeted with sand and pea gravel, and labeled it Quail Hilton.

Both babies snuggled comfortably under the soft feather duster, peeping and peering at us through a skylight of mosquito netting. It was a toss-up whether the dying gasps of Pedro, or Pedra's non-stop healthy cheeps generated more murderous thoughts in me. For that matter, Betsi's insufferable cheerfulness touched raw nerves and I wished for temporary deafness. I said nothing, but stole side-glances at Betsi's smug, beaming face. The cardboard box, jammed tightly between our front seats, scuffed my knuckles every shift up the mountainous desert highway.

"This won't work," I told Betsi. "I can't shift gears without scuffing my knuckles."

Betsi warbled a merry folk song. For her the sun had never shone brighter. She gazed lovingly at her new family and told them, "Your father always is grumpy mornings but his humor improves as the day wears on." The chicks cheeped cheerful agreement.

She tagged my cheek with a swift kiss. "You'll learn to accommodate."

I shuddered at this new defect in her personality. A chirrupy laugh further unsettled my nerves as I eye balled the curving center line and—shifting gears up the winding highway to Flagstaff—scraped my knuckles again.

That Pedro had survived the night remained a minor miracle, for each breath had been an effort. He had stretched under the heat lamp, inattentively waiting for death but had not reckoned with Betsi's talent. Watered Jim Beam carried him throughout the night and he now pecked tentatively at

9

the formula, then sank lazily into the feather duster and slept. "He's resting," Betsi explained.

"He's drunk."

"Don't be silly, he hasn't had a drink in two hours," she countered.

We four drove silently along Interstate 17 except for Pedra's interminable cheeping at my side.

About sixty miles north of Phoenix, we paused at Sunset Point to admire the snow-capped San Francisco peaks ahead and prepare breakfast. A cloth table cover was basic camping equipment and we were renowned for providing bone china cups around sagebrush campfires. It's a small and comforting elegance we enjoyed. Jonquils, heather and pine cones decorate our camping table in season as we carry civilization with us into backwood trails. This morning, in moonlight, Betsi had clipped three fresh hibiscus blooms from the tiny garden to decorate our first breakfast on the road.

In the past, on arrival at any camp, we always shared the work load and usually set a temporary home in about thirty seconds. I carried the ice chest, dishes and chairs. Betsi brought napkins, food and tablecloth. Our routine never varied, so I watched in dismay as Betsi jogged to the picnic site with the cardboard box and set it dead center on our breakfast table. Both birds, disturbed by the move, set up a horrendous protest within their echo chamber and I glanced anxiously about in embarrassment. Betsi didn't seem to hear.

Despondency settled in my stomach. In a parched voice I asked, "Why are you bringing those birds to our breakfast table?"

Betsi's eyes sparkled more than usual and her cheeks flushed pink in the sunrise. "They're family, too," she said, her bubble of enthusiasm nearly bursting. Ignoring me, she searched in the duster and retrieved a tiny speckled bird. "Look!" she directed Pedra, for Pedro still hid inside the feathered bundle. "Look at the desert."

Pedra stared over the cacti, absorbed in a view that tempted wanderers to linger and then return again and again. Her beady eyes darted quickly around and she almost leaped through Betsi's fingers, which was a promising sign. Despite her infancy Pedra possessed incredible speed and I was encouraged how easily she might disappear. I smiled at the possibility.

Fortified by thoughts of escape and her nimble thrust for freedom, I ran to the camper and returned with tea, cake and the hibiscus. Betsi poured from the steel thermos, then clanked her cup at me with an air of rich fulfillment. "To Pedro, our first born since retirement."

"Jeeze," I muttered.

"And to Pedra," she continued, "long may she live." Cheerfully sipping spiced tea, she hummed for joy although I saw nothing but gloomy problems encased in the cardboard apple box.

"I'm too old for another family," I moaned.

Betsi did not sympathize. "Don't cry. You've lived through worse situations."

First-wave landings at Casablanca, Sicily and Anzio crossed my memory, but I had faced those without the apprehension these desert quail now presented. Betsi arose, leaned on the table and made slow, soothing noises into the box while I collected the breakfast gear.

Despite my forebodings, the first day went surprisingly well. Both puff balls peeped incessantly for Pedro had discovered his voice and Betsi, blissfully content, fed them formula hourly while planning college educations and appropriate marriages.

Utah's Coral Sands State Park welcomed us at dusk with brisk weather. The cool, clear night worried Betsi and, at dusk, she plunged the infants deeply into the duster and covered the apple box with a heavy bath towel. Exposure kills many newly hatched quail and thoughts of flash-frozen birds did not appeal to her. Nor did it appeal to me. I would much rather have seen them vanish forever into the creosote patches among the sand dunes. But the sound of their cheeps made Betsi laugh, so they stayed.

At least a million stars filled the sky when evening chill pressed around the camp fire and we huddled closer to its embers. Scrub juniper and desert primrose surrounded us and we stretched comfortably in our deck chairs. I locked my hands behind my head and, eyes nearly closed in lazy contentment, viewed Betsi with grudging admiration. "I'll give you credit for saving Pedro. He nearly died."

Betsi poked a glowing mesquite ember with her marshmallow stick. "Nearly? His interview with St. Peter was almost complete when I picked him up."

The fire's last warmth faded and we pulled parkas closely around our shoulders as mountain chill shocked us with unaccustomed shivers. "I thought he was dead." I confessed, "It's nearly a miracle."

Fatigue overcame Betsi and, barely awake, she peered at tumbling galaxies overhead. "Not at all. Mostly tender loving care. Love," she said as she kicked the fireplace for stray life and opened the camper door, "can do almost anything." Inside, one of the chicks peeped a quiet goodnight and somewhere in the moonlight a nightbird called in the jackpine as we slid into dreamland.

We smelled mountains in Wyoming next day and goosed the camper into extra mileage. In our haste we nearly missed Elbow campground. On previous visits Elbow had earned top honors with us for good reasons. Securely isolated inside mature groves of lodge pole pine and a meandering Snake River, we rated it a nearly perfect campsite. Few campers discovered its beauty and, as usual, we found Elbow deserted and waiting.

Betsi considered herself a fisherman—with ample evidence to support her belief—and had limbered her spinning-rod arm in Sun City just for this moment. She had talked about it for months. Rainbow trout waited in the Snake and fishing tackle lay ready on top of the bed.

Pan-sized trout slapped at Mayflies as we drove in and, with dusk settling inside canyon walls, I readied camp anticipating Betsi's trout catch for dinner, our standard procedure. She usually provided fish before dark and I set my mouth for fresh-lemoned rainbow.

But strangely, she did not reach for her spinning rod. Instead, tugging the metal mesh from the camper she, for the first time, set up the quail motel. Erecting the wire enclosure on uneven ground filled me with happiness for it offered perfect escape routes. Both quail, I surmised, would disappear into the invading darkness within minutes and we would be alone with our can of pork and beans. I could live without fresh fish tonight if that happened. My prayers had been answered.

Happily unaware of the potential danger, Betsi pinned netting on top and funneled the birds, one at a time, into their temporary home. Ecstasy overcame them. Scratching brown sand between their toes, they peeped cheerfully and galloped non-stop around the pen eager for exercise, never pausing at possible escape routes. Their disappointing performance set my teeth on edge, but Betsi viewed her brainchild cage and chicks with delight.

After the pork and bean dinner I rested on my haunches and gazed into the fire for inspiration. In times past, dying embers had supplied answers to vexing problems and I searched around the edge, then into the heart of the flames for suggestions. None came. Aching arthritis seeped into my knees and I rose with difficulty, then sank into the softer camp chair still waiting for answers from the shifting embers. But tonight they were non-communicative and, while waiting for a final sign, a great horned owl hooted in the darkened timber. I had never understood their lonesome repetitive language, so my eyes drifted closed and I thought and thought and thought. Someplace, somewhere, somehow I would rid my camp of two Gambel's quail.

Crisp mountain air set a frown on Betsi's face, for she knew exposure could result in chilly deaths for the infants. She pulled a chocolate bar from her parka pocket and unwrapped it carefully. "Remember those cold Montana nights when we were kids? We'd heat bricks in the oven and wrap them in towels for our cold beds. We can do the same for the children." She clapped her hands in self congratulation and shoved a softball-sized granite boulder near the embers. "That's our firebrick," she said.

Later, after tucking the quail into their feathery bed, she carefully wrapped the gray boulder in a sweater and pressed it near the duster. Both chicks cheeped appreciatively. "How's that for mountain life?" she asked them. "Tomorrow we'll buy you sleeping bags."

We scrambled into bed and kissed goodnight, gazing through open windows into the cosmos and, surrounded by towering black mountains and the rushing Snake River, we reviewed our busy day. Only falling stars disrupted our reverie and, so closely did they apparently streak toward us in lazy dying arcs that Betsi stretched her long fingers to intercept them. Then both of us shook imaginary sparks from our sleeping bags and laughed at our silliness. We fell asleep with the whisper of pine needles rustling about us and the Snake River swirling around glacier-smoothed rocks barely twenty feet away.

Morning fog filled the canyon road to Jackson, Wyoming and, lights on, the dependable VW twisted slowly down the highway. The VW was our sixth or seventh in an evolutionary line of campers. Over the years we had owned tarps and tents, converted vans, a trailer and one extraordinarily dismal failure—an ornate expensive motor home—for we were mountain campers. On a wintry Sunday morning through sheer good fortune we corrected that judgment error. Wandering through a snowy deserted used-car lot in Montana, Betsi spotted the nearly new immaculate red camper. Both of us gasped at its beauty although we had never seriously considered one previously. We bought it Monday morning before the salesman opened his till. We never regretted the purchase and sold the monstrous motor home at a tidy profit.

Nearing its hundred-thousandth mile birthday, the camper never failed us. Following two major operations in local garages for abdominal pains, it now carried us joyfully through mountains and deserts. It bore us up torturous mountain passes, along flowering meadows and tranquil pastures and, thrilled by these bounties, we frequently broke into song. We sang long-forgotten childhood diddies off-key and yodelled western ballads while riding across snow-covered ranges. Frequently at high noon we corkscrewed into tight openings along shady streams and munched fresh fruit and cheese.

The camper gracefully tolerated our high spirits, tone deafness and capricious whims. At times we suddenly waved at working farmers in fields and tapped its tin horn loudly in triumphant tatoo. Now, approaching Jackson, the camper seemed to share Betsi's joy and enthusiasm for it raced forward rapidly like a spirited stallion and plunged from dense fog into sunshine and promise. Only I remained apprehensive. 🐦

Chapter Three

The weekly Jackson flea market sparkled with activity. A crowded poultry cage sporting nervous live chickens, ducks and one plump turkey rested on grass alongside fresh gladiolas and rose buds. A small rosy-cheeked child sat cross-legged, intently fashioning a dandelion chain, her tongue peeping through tightened lips. The singing hum of happy voices flowed over the square and six or eight children ran through the busy market in a game of tag. Spare tires, fresh sweet corn, velvet art and old clothing spilled over well-used card tables. I browsed through a used-book collection while Betsi poked into bins of worn clothing. Neither of us sighted miniature sleeping bags.

Slowing in front of a table overflowing with granola, tofu and fresh alfalfa sprouts, Betsi paused. A youthful shiny-scrubbed woman abruptly interrupted a conversation about yogurt and kelp with her neighbor and turned instantly to Betsi. Her bleached floral print feed-sack dress covered sturdy feet braced for the first sale of the day. "What're you looking for?"

"Do you have any woolen socks?"

"Oh yes. Several pair, if you can find the correct size." The smiling free spirit smoothed her handmade lace collar and tugged a stuffed cardboard box from under the table. "Some of these should fit," she said.

Betsi pawed through the clump and tossed a pair of heavy gray woolen socks on the table. "How much?" she asked with feigned disinterest, for Betsi passionately believed in the art of bargaining as she believed in Milk of Magnesia and bittersweet chocolate. But she had misjudged her adversary.

The willowy young lady stopped arranging her stack of alfalfa sprouts, glanced up and sighed. "I'm afraid these won't be satisfactory. They're much too large for you and they have holes in the toes."

15

Betsi inhaled several breaths of Wyoming air in astonishment. She had not expected honesty. "Size isn't important," she said. "How much?"

The earth mother's sense of fair play continued and her blue eyes flashed. "They're too big and have holes in them," she repeated firmly.

Betsi could not bargain with honesty. Defeated, she said, "I think they're exactly what I want. How much?"

The flower child shrugged her shoulders. "If you insist, twenty-cents and I'll loan you yarn.

Betsi continued fishing in the sock box and hooked a smaller pair from the pile. She thrust them toward the girl. "How much for these?"

The entrepreneur smiled as though chiding a child for eating mud pies. "Lady," the girl said, "One pair is too large, the other is too small and both have holes in them. They're only good for scrap yarn."

It had been a long time since anyone called Betsi "lady" and the compliment completely humbled her. Raising her eyes, she asked, "How much for both pair? I'll pay what they're worth."

A sigh of resignation shook the hippie. "I'll throw them in with the first pair if you'll take darning yarn to mend them."

It had not been the challenging transaction Betsi had anticipated. She paid the girl and took the socks and yarn. "I'm really not interested in old socks," the girl confided. "How about some fresh tofu?"

Betsi lifted her eyes to mine as if to say, "I knew I couldn't trust her completely. Tofu!!" But the accusation remained unspoken. "No tofu. Not today," Betsi told her firmly and we left the perplexed young lady shaking her head. Betsi waved the socks at me. "Our quail sleeping bags!" she squealed jubilantly. "Four bags. Now the babies will always have clean bedding."

Only a few miles away meadowlarks trilled at us from hidden ground nests and juniper campfire smoke drifted along the wooden rail fence line in Gros Ventre campground. Mysterious sunlit clouds announced the Grand Tetons stretching sky ward directly ahead. We would meet them intimately in a few days and, except for the chattering, excited quail at my elbow, a carefree golden summer lay within our grasp.

My magic dream was not to be however, for the quail demanded full-time attention. Wasting no time in establishing priorities, Betsi briskly set up their cage first, fed and watered them, then pulled her chair within inches of the birds and stared proudly as if coveting a pile of gold bullion. But their demand for food and lodging sank into oblivion compared to screams of anguish when she disappeared from sight. I shall never forget the first time Betsi left us alone while searching for the bathroom.

I had chopped firewood and was stretched out on cool grass. Light mountain breezes brushed through camp and a peregrine falcon—or was it an osprey? I couldn't tell, it soared so high, sailed lazily in the warm rising current. The bird appeared to be only a speck in the clouds as I continued deep satisfying breathing and wound my fingers around prairie grasses in warm damp earth. The smell of mushrooms and decaying bark filtered around me, for mountain smells are stronger and more satisfying than most. Temporarily I enjoyed peace, for the quail stalked within their cage and, finding it well stocked with food, squeaked satisfaction in low throaty sounds.

Next door a pair of young lovers seemed disposed to thunderous, hard rock music and public display of affection as they tumbled and tossed on a double air mattress. A monumental stack of empty beer cans surrounded them and they blended into late-morning oblivion of beer and passion. I watched with modest interest, recalling similar personal frolics more than fifty years ago. Betsi, too, scanned the couple with amused detachment and, with a flutter of her skirt, announced, "I'm going to the bathroom."

No sooner had she disappeared than the quail stopped eating, and, searching for Betsi, set off an alarm. Pedro streaked around the cage in a curious crab-like marathon while Pedra flapped her wings in despair. Both frantically eyeballed the campground for Betsi while circling the cage. A cacophony of quail protests filled the air. So sharp and demanding was the sound that the startled lovers halted in midair, flicked off the transistor and stared as though a bomb had dropped in their laps. A passing camper driving along, stopped, rolled down his windows and listened with wonderment before nearly driving off the road. The falcon, high above, peeled into a cloud and shrank from the noise.

"My God," I thought, "how can two peanut-sized babies produce such an uproar?" Self-pity overwhelmed me and I thought silently, "Is this going to be our life all summer? Can we honestly allow two quail infants to ruin our tranquility?" The tumbling questions rolled to a stop and a single bold answer surfaced. "No, by God, no! Enough is too much of anything. The quail must go. Now!"

As though punctuating my thoughts, both screaming infants bombarded the netting in a series of desperate escape attempts and intensified their cries. Violent trembling came over me and I clasped my head tightly with both hands trying to control my temper. Betsi trotted briskly into camp. "What have you been doing with my babies?" she asked with a broad smile. "I could hear them down in the rest room." (They could have been heard in Timbuktu.)

She was in high humor with their performance and at the sound of her voice both birds ceased scrambling and dropped to the ground as quickly as they'd risen. Their intense caterwauling diminished to soft, contented welcoming cheeps, their voices akin to a squeaky rubber toy, and they scratched innocently among grasses. The tranquil, domestic scene before me revealed an amazing contrast to the horrid screams of desperation only seconds ago. The lovers cautiously strummed a guitar and nuzzled each other in exploratory fashion, the falcon reappeared through the clouds and traffic pressed uninterrupted across camp. Both birds chattered and scratched with obscene guiltlessness, but my blood pressure soared with the floating osprey high above us.

I wasted no time and, diplomatically as possible, told Betsi, "Those damned birds have to go. I'm not spending another night under the same roof."

Betsi studied my tight lips, white face, bristling tone and, with years of patient understanding, said, "You're right as usual. They are a problem. What shall we do with them?"

"I don't care," I sputtered. "Get rid of them. Now!"

"How? Shall we simply turn them loose for coyotes or snakes? That osprey upstairs is looking for breakfast" She raised her blue eyes and with a false helpless look that turned my vertebrae to marshmallows, tilted her head sideways in defeat.

Reason slowly returned and I began disciplining murderous thoughts. No easy solution surfaced, so I stomped into the camper muttering evil incantations.

That evening in Gros Ventre camp, Betsi carefully enlarged toe holes in the woolen socks and invited Pedro to climb inside. He stared at the sock opening as if he had just been presented a French menu. After a moment and a couple of encouraging shoves, he tunneled his way through the sock into the toe and peered at us rather enthusiastically. Sealing the opposite end with a ponytail elastic, Betsi presented him to me as carefully as if he was the Hope diamond.

"I know you won't mind holding your son a few minutes," she told me cheerfully. "He won't bite." I did mind, but accepted him because the afternoon had been intensely quiet.

Pedro, never at loss for words, squinted at me and cheeped so enthusiastically that I was tempted to answer, but quickly reminded myself that I did not talk to birds. My silence did not concern him at all and he continued chattering in a most provocative manner, scratching a comfortable nest inside his sock and settling down, bubbling with conversation and goodwill. His voice rose in volume, then he suddenly stopped in the middle of his soliloquy and stared at me as though asking a question. Before I quite realized what I was doing, I answered him.

I don't remember my reply, but it satisfied Pedro and he continued visiting in pleasant tones. Slightly embarrassed with our conversation, I lowered my voice and replied only in gruff monosyllables. Pedro did not seem to notice my reluctance to visit with him or accept our threadbare relationship. Instead he stared into the campfire, then turned to me as though I was Einstein. Satisfied all was well, he snuggled deeply into my fist, tossing pleasant confidential messages in my direction. He chatted continuously and I simply found it easier to agree than disagree. Listening to his pleasant discussion I grudgingly admitted that a gratifying experience lay in my hand and warmth spread through me that had not been present since our early morning blow-up. Even so, I staunchly vowed to renew my battle for independence at sunrise.

Pedra, however, did not share Pedro's flair for cooperation. When Betsi nudged her little bird toward the sock, she met instant resistance. Tiny sharp toes braced against Betsi's palm and Pedra's head darted furiously from side to side. She snapped rapidly at Betsi. She did not want to be

19

confined. Half turning, she leaped for freedom, but Betsi pressed her deeply into the woolen bag. Frantically and in a spasm of spirit, Pedra squirted around again and nearly escaped between Betsi's trembling fingers.

Pedro and I watched the fluttering skirmish with interest, for victory was undecided until Betsi oozed the baby through the entire length and pushed her head through the opening. Surprised, Pedra jerked her eyes toward us, nodded to the campfire and signaled a temporary truce. Exhausted in defeat she dozed in front of the sagebrush embers, roused temporarily when Betsi offered two ants as a reward for her doubtful cooperation. Drifting into a cooing slumber, her bright dark eyes popped open suddenly flashing a warning that she would not be an easy child to rear. Then she dozed again.

So bedtime routine was established. The chicks loved the warmth and security of woolen socks. Mesmerized by firelight they watched ashes glow and, firmly secure in sleeping bags, they yawned widely and dozed in our hands until we bedded them in the apple box. There they peacefully remained until next morning.

Betsi continued placing the padded warm rock in bed on crisp nights, but it was unnecessary since the woolen socks provided ample mountain-chill protection. But she took no chances. She held the greatest affection for the oddest things and I watched her eyes follow the rock as though it were gold, realizing with hernia pain that, as long as the birds remained in camp, the burden of a ten pound granite boulder would remain part of our camping gear.

After bedding the quail we usually returned to the fire for conversation and hot chocolate. One evening Betsi struck at the fading coals with a willow stick and sparks exploded like a hatch of frightened fireflies. Embers snapped and a sudden tiny flame burst from the glowing heap illuminating Betsi's somber face. "I told you we could work this out." She spoke more to the dying fire than to me but I remained unconvinced.

Even so, nightly campfires, (unbelievably we had been in Gros Ventre a solid week) with its scent of pungent sage smoke, tightened us into an intimate circle of love and friendship.

Daylight provided us little leisure time. Happy hours flowed through our fingers as Betsi shifted the quail crib hourly to shady spots, washed clothes and cooked. When we left camp, the infant birds accompanied us (inside their sleeping bags), tucked in our pockets or daypacks. Each day we planned hikes, visits to old familiar sites and later, always, campfires. Pocket books lay unread. We rose earlier and bedded later yet always faced a full tomorrow.

One evening as Betsi readied the birds for sleep, I nodded at an Indian paintbrush blooming in a drifting moon shadow. "We're committed," I said aloud to the flower. "There's no turning back." But I glanced over my shoulder at the rising moon for an escape route.

So despite my overwhelming misgivings, within two short weeks a quiet pervasive happiness crept into our hearts. I had never seen Betsi happier and, monitored by the Grand Tetons ahead and, warmed by evening pine cone fires, we plotted our tomorrows, Pedra and Pedro always included.

Chapter Four

The tone of our temporary truce changed abruptly at 1:18 Monday afternoon on a shopping trip to Jackson. I remember glancing at my watch as Betsi stumbled and fell sprawling on the wooden walk. The exact time, for some odd reason, seemed more indelibly fixed in memory than her terrified cry of pain. Lying on the sidewalk in a fetal spasm she glanced up, tight lips puckered, preventing another outcry, then quietly whispered, "I'm really hurt!"

A crowd gathered. We never explained her fall. It was nearly high noon, remarkably clear, and bone-dry. We never blamed the wooden-planked sidewalk in Jackson either. We had safely walked its rustic surface many years and so considered her accident an act of God, but never blamed Him either. Now Betsi lay contorted in a knot of pain begging us not to touch her.

Six-hundred-and-three dollars later, an X-ray and the emergency room physician confirmed no broken bones, but a severe ankle sprain, pulled muscles, a badly bruised elbow and torn ligaments in her chest. She left the hospital, tightly bandaged and sporting new maple crutches.

Inside the camper, Betsi began to cry silently as her eyes shifted from her bandages to the quail box to me. Then her hand reached over and grasped mine. Long gasping sobs wracked her body and I thought she cried out in pain. Finally she quieted and whimpered, "What are we going to do with the quail?"

She sat quietly for a moment, her auburn hair, flecked with silver, rumpled but still attractive since she always kept it short during camping season. She pushed a brief smile past her thin lips and sad inquiring eyes and I decided her beauty had blossomed during twenty years of marriage. Then, without thinking, I said, "I'll take care of the quail."

She looked directly into my eyes and said, as a cold-blooded fact, "You hate those birds. And you know it."

I waited a moment before answering, for there was a ring of truth in her accusation. Yet, I rationalized, if I truly hated them they would not be alive today. "Noooooo." Words did not come easily. "I don't exactly hate them, but I don't exactly love them, either. About the same rating as brussel sprouts."

"You flush brussel sprouts down the garbage disposal," she refreshed my memory.

"But I learned to eat them," I said. "I can learn to put up with the quail."

"I know you hate those birds," she insisted.

"But I love you and you need quail therapy. I'll take care of your birds."

She studied my face, and under the circumstances, saw a rare form of sincerity. "I knew you would." She knuckled a tear from her cheek. "Let's go to the Tetons. Let's go to Coulter Bay." To seal the bargain, she tightened her grip around my wrist so fiercely that I winced in pain.

Memories of Jim Bridger's ghost and his Indian wives followed us into Coulter Bay campground. Throughout our lives we frequently enjoyed the enchanted paradise, for we had lived only two hundred miles from Grand Teton National Park. Time had been our great enemy then, and now, with retirement dreams stretched in front of us, we determined to explore as long as we wished. Nothing, it seemed, could prevent that dream. Nothing except two disruptive, wild Gambel's quail and a crutch-hobbling wife.

But Betsi refused defeat and her brainchild, the sturdy wire pen, greatly simplified my life. It proved wonderfully adapted to camping. Easily erected, the enclosure insured important scratching ground and dust bath areas. After incarceration in the apple box the elation of freedom uncorked quail springs in their legs and they repeatedly popped, Zulu-like, inside the cage when released. I noted with increasing uneasiness their frenzied flutterings to the top of the wire fence. Now I dare not let them escape! Illusions of introducing Gambel's quail into the Tetons cluttered my mind and I doubled efforts to prevent escape. It was a case of hell if I did and hell if I didn't, with me in dead center.

I always located the cage on fairly level earth and tent-staked it into the ground. A small log or rock was set in the center since the birds seemed to enjoy penthouse views. After securing the mosquito-netting top, I carried the will-o'-the-wisp puffs from the apple box. Only six inches separated the box from the cage, but every transfer claimed hours from my life for the squiggly babes squirmed like greased pigs. I dared not squeeze too hard for fear of fracturing delicate bones, yet a positive grip was absolutely necessary. Betsi directed each transfer of prisoners with an authoritative sweep of her crutches.

One at a time, I dropped the chicks inside like dollops of pancake batter and quickly locked the small net entrance. Once secure, the quail squirted around the pen seeking freedom. Then Betsi and her crutches relaxed.

After futilely searching for escape routes both birds pranced within the enclosure, pecking and chirping. Pedro always leaped onto the penthouse and surveyed the Teton range. Gentle fields of lupine and Western paintbrush surrounded him and he seemed satisfied. He was never disturbed by moose browsing at nearby Jackson Lake, but occasionally cocked an alert eye toward the noble snow-capped mountains.

But Pedra was different! Wild breezes from Mt. Moran swept through the wire pen and rolled snippets of twigs across the dirt floor. Pedra attacked each moving piece, tossing it into the air only stopping from time to time to critically examine Jackson Lake below. Sometimes she seemed to disapprove of its calmness, the slight riffles on shore or its very existence. We were never certain about her temperamental whims. She pecked and swallowed minute grains of sand, but flung larger pieces backward over her head into a discard heap. Her impatient blood brooked no foolishness and she glanced sideways, continuously chiding Pedro for imaginary faults. Even Betsi rolled her eyes skyward at their obvious differences.

Quail formula remained their staple diet, although Betsi experimented with other food. Their continuous gluttony produced hundreds of spiny pin feathers and large, hot feet. Both welcomed small insects, medium-sized grasshoppers, spiders and green worms into the cage. One night a hatch of damselflies elevated them to a level of ecstasy.

The fluttering hatch appeared as if by magic on a calm evening. Pedro rested atop his perch and Pedra stalked beneath him scolding and scratching. Suddenly the cage filled with newly-hatched damselflies. Both chicks snapped instinctively at the flying insects. They ate one, then another, and yet more. It was only the beginning! In a frenzy—often crashing into each other—they bounded about the cage devouring the delicacy as though each conquest was the last insect on earth. We had never seen them so excited. Fifteen minutes later thousands of damselflies remained but both birds as well as Betsi and myself faced exhaustion. None of us could have eaten another damselfly. The baby quail, craws stuffed to overflowing, sank together completely replete while Betsi and I confessed we seldom had experienced a more entertaining evening.

At Coulter Bay campground, Betsi's aches slowly and painfully subsided. Torn chest muscles would remind her of Jackson for months. Torn ligaments would heal at snail's pace and did not respond to Milk of Magnesia. Frustrated, she hobbled about camp breathing slowly and carefully.

It was Betsi who discovered the quail's hot feet. At first she thought they had a fever until a ranger at the information center told us quail body temperatures varied between 105 and 111 degrees. Our quail seemed to concentrate all heat in their oversized feet. Only after a dust bath did they cool off, but the rest of the time Betsi claimed she could fry—well, at least coddle—eggs on their toes.

They peeped quietly as evening approached and huddled together as friends. Pedra, almost as large as her brother, pushed under his immature wing. Although it was impossible to find protection there, she hovered and thrust at him, desperately seeking warmth. The futility of finding security under his sparse pin feathers apparently never occurred to her. Yet she struggled for his warmth and protection night after night. He never objected.

The bird's quick adaptation to their sleeping bags fired Betsi's zeal and after a night or two they scurried without protest deeply into the socks. Their tiny heads poked outward waiting for campfire programs, hot chocolate and conversation. Truly, they enjoyed the woolen cocoons and even pushed toward the heat-soaked rock, for it was much cooler in Coulter Bay. Both birds seemed ready for sunset, their energies depleted and with little defense against darkness, they welcomed sleeping bags, a warm fire and our company. When penned inside the box they remained quiet until morning unless nightmares caused a single quick and frantic call in the middle of the night.

Mindless quail dreams disturbed us initially, for they came suddenly and always in the deep quiet of darkness. Both birds suffered midnight heebie-jeebies. Betsi twisted painfully from her tangled sleeping bag at the first frantic cry and plunged a shaft of light into their box searching for a wandering coyote or hungry grizzly bear, but the startled quail stared absent-mindedly at her, apparently having forgotten the source of their fright. The cry did seem desperate, coming as it did without reason, for it was a distinctive single, high-piercing call, which was never repeated and never occurred on successive nights. After several hair-raising wakenings we labelled them nightmares and probably caused by small pizza pieces at bedtime or too many ant larvae. Subsequently, when a sharp wolf-like howl originated from the apple box, Betsi cooed soft, comforting words and the quail answered a few consoling clucks and fell asleep before we did.

Our quail were daytime birds. Both remained silent until dawn then, hearing us rise and prepare breakfast, cheeped quiet morning welcomes. They gratefully accepted Betsi's spoon-fed formula while still inside their socks, sometimes cocking a darting head skyward to determine the weather outside, but never anxious to leave the warmth of their feather duster or sleeping bags. Cold mountain soil and frigid alpine mornings held no charm for either baby.

The disastrous shock of quail ownership slowly subsided under Betsi's patient guidance and Pedro's increasing attraction for me. But I had little time for leisure. I was an early riser with little regard for temperature. Both quail and Betsi arose late and abhorred cold, so morning almost disappeared by the time breakfast dishes were finished. When lunch came, the pen had to be moved to a shady spot in the heat of the day, for they did not enjoy full summer sun either. Then we moved them yet again, for by the time their bed was cleaned and new dirt placed inside, the sun had rolled forward. Days vanished and, although my skill as quail-sitter improved, the quail consumed most waking hours. I began to look forward to bedtime as much as the birds. Skirmishes with Betsi's determination in the past had proved fruitless and her quail madness—plus my promise—strengthened her authority. So, while I no longer prayed for a quailless household aloud, I would have welcomed His assistance in making our golden years more tranquil.

Actually I enjoyed watching Pedro snake into his sock, squeeze through the entire length and burst from the toe-hole in triumph. For, with evening shadows crossing camp, he came to my hand willingly, ready to begin the evening's chatter. I confess he gave me certain satisfaction. His warm feet, rapt attention, and snuggling into my palm settled my nerves. I wouldn't tell Betsi that a gentle affection had developed between us, but she may have suspected it, for I no longer grumbled when he arrived in his nightclothes. I reluctantly accepted that camping with quail might not be the tragedy I had forecast.

But their daily daytime tantrums bothered both of us—as well as neighbors—for one could not easily ignore their thunderous protests when Betsi left camp. Public nuisance eviction threatened us each time the park ranger drove past. We shuddered at his approach and our fluttering nerves twitched to fibrilating pitch at the arrival of an unleashed German shepherd sniffing and snorting around the cage. He could have consumed both birds in a single gulp!

Yet we did not protest the dog, for we knew wild quail were not classified proper pets within the Park. Neither did we want to leave. Two weeks was a small time to devote to Coulter Bay, and our Tetons. Many pleasures awaited us at Jenny lake, Menor's Ferry and Jackson Hole as Betsi's injuries continued improving. Yet, after each verbal tantrum Betsi considered muzzling the quail. I threatened strangulation.

About ten days into our stay at Coulter Bay the quail staged a monumental exhibition. When Betsi disappeared for her morning shower, the quail, impatient as hungry tigers, commenced pacing, then burst into a cacophony of wild shrieks. Their protests exceeded all previous performances and I considered awarding Oscars to them on the spot. In desperation they caterwauled non-stop, flinging themselves against the wire, bruising wingtips and destroying emerging feathers. I expected, and prayed for, death from exhaustion before Betsi returned, but they mustered enough strength for further assaults on my sanity. Together they trilled blasphemies at Jackson Lake and the Grand Teton itself. Avalanches had been triggered with less cause and I prepared for crashes from across the lake.

Horrified, I watched the Ranger's pickup cruise toward us. Simultaneously the German shepherd loped within ten feet and stared stiff-legged, tail poker straight, his bright darting eyes fixed on the vocally eruptive quail. Betsi hobbled to camp as rapidly as possible, her crutches flinging dust and gravel along the road while rubbing her frizzled wet hair with a heavy bath towel.The cold water shower and shampoo, enhanced her facial color and she limped swiftly to her birds.

"Have you been pinching my babies?" Her flat humor faded when she sensed the atmosphere. The ranger's pickup skidded to a halt in front of us. The shepherd moved within five feet of the cage and sat open-mouthed at the spectacle. I did not need to explain the situation to Betsi.

The panic-stricken birds, welded into a coil of terror from which death seemed the only answer, caught sight of Betsi and dropped to the ground, their throats vibrating in rapid last-gasp puffs. Penetrating wails chastised her for clearly they never expected to see their mother again. They had been orphaned! Slowly, their sharp cries lessened and moans of despair modulated into whispering whimpers and—like a run-down gramophone—the laments faded. Calm cooing replaced calls of terror. It was the lull after the storm.

When the last stone spun beneath the skidding wheels of the ranger's truck, he faced a scene of complete tranquility. Pedro chatted with Betsi, lifting his head this way and that, offering small confidential comments on his behavior. Pedra buried herself in a patch of fresh weeds, cooing delightedly at its succulence. The German shepherd waved his tail and contented amazement crept over his face. His tail wagged, his legs relaxed and his eyes requested permission to move forward to examine the birds in greater detail. I nodded and he moved a step closer toward the amazing chatterboxes.

The ranger-naturalist slammed his pickup door and strode rapidly in our direction, his eyes fixed on the birds. "Wild Gambel's quail, aren't they?"

Betsi stared silently ahead. I stirred my tea, withdrew the hot spoon and wiped it on my pants. Slowly I lifted the cup and sipped through steam. We were caught red-handed. "Yes, they're pets. Got them when they were only a day old."

An excited smile flickered across the ranger's face as though an unexpected gift had dropped in his lap. He fell to his knees in front of the cage. "I knew it," he almost screamed. "You can't mistake the sound of a Gambel's. I grew up in Tucson and we had them in our yard." He bent closer and fussed at the fledglings. "God, how I miss these little beauties!"

Poking a finger into the pen, he started talking in low, brief confidential gurgles. He pantomimed into the cage and tapped his finger against the wire. Strangely, the birds responded. Pedro answered him quickly then more slowly Pedra lifted her head from the weeds and walked to him. "See," he shouted with a squeal of laughter, "they understand me!" Like a proud father viewing offspring through glass windows he chattered and cooed at the bemused birds. Both quail listened politely at first, then returned to food, pecking and scratching. The ranger did not notice. He perched on his knees consumed with memories, continuing quail talk as though to old friends.

A second wind returned him to reality. "That your dog?" We shook our heads. "Should be leashed in the park. Could hurt the quail, too." He stood and stretched, gazing fondly at his new little friends. "Aren't they wonderful?" Betsi beamed and nodded vigorous agreement while I remained neutral. "Don't worry. I'll take care of the dog." Then turning again to the quail, he promised,"Don't you worry little guys." The friendly dog followed him to the pickup and the official whistled him inside. Obediently the dog leaped in and both wheeled away.

What desperately long minutes they had been! Our voices slowly returned and Betsi, still drying her hair, clutched a crutch tightly. "I'll take the birds every time I leave," she said.

"How?"

"In their sleeping bags. Same as at night."

Suddenly I felt immensely grateful for her abundant supply of common sense, mostly hidden in a quagmire of Betsi-logic, but dramatically surfacing in a pinch. I squeezed her hand in congratulation. "The birds go with us," I agreed.

And that's the way it happened. Her ankle dramatically improved. We carried them, encased in woolen-sock mummy bags, in our hands, parkas or even shirt pockets, but always with us. We carried them across Jenny Lake, boated the Snake River and walked to nightly fireside talks. They apparently applauded the innovation and seemed sincerely interested in everything. They anticipated every new venture. When we planned an outing, they crept eagerly into their socks, even during the day, ready for any trip.

Just after lunch following the ranger confrontation, we watched a Jeep Wagoneer, towing a tiny trailer chockablock with sleeping bags, ice chests and children, pause at our doorstep. We should have noticed, but one occupant seemed so natural we mistook him for another adult. It was our old friend, the curious German shepherd, who sat between the front seats, looking eagerly through the windshield. The brood of children stacked at random between sleeping bags and clothing filled the rear. When the doors opened the dog leaped out as tour guide and, glancing backward to assure that everyone followed, came to our table, tail wagging and eyes sparkling. Five children and two bedraggled parents followed. I had the feeling of watching a circus act. Although they were pressed for time, at the ranger's urging, the mother told us they could not leave until the children met Pedra and Pedro. And we met King.

All the children hovered around, not quite touching the cage, as the birds scratched and exercised, then, craws filled, they stopped and chatted as though over a backyard fence. Squeals and giggles filled the campsite and the quail, stimulated by new interests, fluttered and pranced. King remained sitting in the rear of the family circle, proudly displaying his discovery. Within minutes, the tribe headed north. Heady with excitement, King rode high in the front seat, his nose pressed tightly against the windshield, guiding the family to Morning Glory Pool and Old Faithful Geyser.

King's brood of seven, as we came to identify them, were not the first nor last visitors. The ranger took daily communion with the birds and our site became Coulter Bay's social center. Everyone seemed to know the birds by name. Small children barely able to walk stumbled through camp asking for Pedra and Pedro. On hiking trails strangers called friendly hellos, by name, to the quail perching in their mummy bags high in our daypacks watching every bend of the path. They seemed vitally interested in all of the Tetons.

We occupied many waking moments explaining our quail. They never needed introductions for their reputations preceded them, but early one day something happened that put socializing completely out of mind.

It was dead quiet that Sunday morning, so still I could barely hear pine needles scraping against the camper. Across Jackson Lake a wild mallard called softly, sounding as though he were in bed beside me. Uphill, smoke rose straight into the awakening sky from an early campfire, and although I heard bacon sizzling, no odor came my way. Betsi snored easily and the quail played dead in their night box as chilly morning temperatures still prevailed. Gently, as though fearful of disturbing the Sabbath, a pervasive scratching filtered around the camper. Peeking through the window I spotted two golden-breasted ground squirrels investigating camp. Visitors had arrived for breakfast.

We never understood why the almond-eyed squirrels chose us, but they did. Neither quail returned their friendship. After breakfast both birds reacted to the squirrels as mortal enemies. Parading in cautious reconnaissance inside the cage, the soup of suspicion thickened and objections to our new neighbors boiled over. The quail leaped high in the pen trying to flee through the closed top. Dropping in a hurricane of twigs and grass they attempted, we presumed, to frighten the ground squirrels, but the furry neighbors only edged closer as the birds tumbled about in a tornado of dust and small gravel, squawking loudly. We had not noticed but the squirrels had apparently crossed the invisible color line.

Betsi, who reasoned that any family enemy became her own enemy, immediately volunteered her services as artillery brigade commander and gathered hillocks of pebbles to barrage the intruders. The fat squirrels immediately recognized game rules and investigated each stone she threw, returning to her for the next toss. A persistent but notoriously poor shot, Betsi had a sore arm by nightfall and the panting squirrels rested on their haunches in near exhaustion.

Early in the relationship, our quail decided that two ground squirrels were plenty. Our new neighbors did not agree and next morning half a dozen more bright-eyed plump cousins circled the cage ready for the great stone-throwing game. Apparently they enjoyed Betsi's recreational activity, for they stuck fast to camp despite her lack of hospitality. Betsi and both quail roared insults at them and throughout the day pegged ever larger stones in their direction. But the squirrels, with quick tail flicks and zig-zag dashes toward the rolling pebbles, did not leave. They liked us!

Next day they became impressive nuisances. Packing Pedra, Pedro and a picnic lunch, we drove to Menor's Ferry early morning and returned to ruinous conditions. The slant-eyed squirrels had burrowed under the cage and eaten every morsel within the crib. They had leaped on the netting trampoline-style and shredded it beyond repair, and now circled us like Oriental Indians around a besieged wagon train. We watched them hover closer and closer and, one by one, dart to the cage springing against it making rapid scratches into the earth. Betsi's ammunition, inaccurately thrown, only frightened the quail, and the squirrels seemed delighted with our return. They apparently had missed us. That night we raised the white flag and decided to evacuate. Time had come for our quail to experience new territory and meet my mother. ➤

Chapter Five

Mother moved west in 1909. Billings, Montana, claimed to be an authentic cowtown and it was. She watched dusty paths develop into oil-sprinkled roads. Cobblestone streets that buckled like a camel's hump during rainstorms came next and finally, honest to God streets—macadam, residents called them—with rubber stop-signs embedded directly in the center of each intersection. Clanging traffic signals emerged, one at a time, much later. Widowed, she reared four boys on a 5-acre truck farm and when they grew into manhood and great grandchildren reached puberty, mother expressed surprise she had become old. Celebrating her eightieth birthday she told friends about her relief at reaching that age. "I lost so many friends in the dangerous seventies," she lamented.

Tough, work-hardened skin stretched over her arthritic fingers. Her gall bladder disappeared early in life as did her appendix, tonsils and adenoids in a rash of minor surgeries. Mother never saw a doctor for a cold or an ache. She needed an operating table before she called for help and she delivered all four boys on the family four-poster. She owned a steel hip, a patched eardrum and gained multiple contusions through exploratory diggings. One day she broke her arm cranking the model-T Ford, for self-starters were not known then. While digging a water-well, the earth caved in about her and so did four crushed ribs, yet she continued cooking, gardening and collecting opinions. Mother bragged that she never had been jailed, but was cited once for driving too slowly on the interstate highway. Merry eyes dimmed and hearing faded, but her zest for living and good humor never flagged. Her memory sharpened with age. At least no one challenged facts as she shouted them. She was only five feet tall when she married and, over the years, shrank an inch or two. "I've never had time to grow up," she told us.

Untamed by years, she neither swore nor drank but came close when the Yankees lost baseball games and when Jack Kennedy became president. A Missouri Democrat, she lost faith in that party, for the Kennedys overwhelmed her. Explosive pooh poohs shouted down Kennedy's admirers as she pointed an arthritic finger at all who would listen. "Don't ever trust that man!" mother shouted. She never did, but mourned his death.

Mother disliked President Johnson more than she mistrusted Kennedy and never again voted a Democratic ticket. "I've lived too long," she told me one afternoon. "They don't make Democrats like they used to." Oppressively silent during Watergate, she fled to her garden and hoed weeds vigorously for two years, placing her faith in the Yankees and avoiding all political opinions. Those years, in the neighborhood, were known as the "quiet ones". Subsequently she based America's progress on Yankee win-loss statistics and the year the Yanks lost a close pennant race she told me in all sincerity, "This country really is going to the dogs."

Mother's year began in February. That's when seed catalogs arrived in the roadside mailbox. Those multicolored brochures offered hope for the future and a reason for her existence. She copied long detailed lists in neat backhand and ordered seeds early. When they arrived she planted tiny seeds in half-gallon milk containers and stored them under her bed. Subsequently she transplanted the seedlings and pressed them tightly into her kitchen window. After that the entire house filled with fragrant plants. Shortly the Yankees began spring training and mother was off and running, or as fast as she could at eighty-six with a game hip.

So we were not surprised at her instant acceptance of the birds, for she enjoyed most things, but her physical deterioration since last year alarmed us. Half a dozen hand magnifying lenses lay conveniently about the house and she verified objects with quick peeks through them. Her artificial hip, implanted in ancient days, chronically ached and she limped with the aid of a diamond-willow cane. Yet she only complained about the loss of her driver's license. Lack of independence troubled her, for she knew it was terminal.

She had mentioned hearing loss in years past, but accurately interpreted all small background whispers. Therefore, we believed her hearing equal to ours. Finally, I suspected her deafness to be real when I introduced Pedra. Lifting both quail in their socks I said, "Mother, here are your newest great-grandchildren. This is Pedra."

"Harold," she shouted with her high quivering voice. "That's a nice name. Boy quail, eh? Boys run in the family, you know."

"No, mother. Pedra's a girl."

"No matter," she said. "Harold's still a nice name. What's the other one called?"

"His name is Pedro."

"Hatrack!" she yelled. "Now that's different. Nice, but different. Boy or girl?"

"Pedro's a boy quail."

She nodded. "Good. You need a pair. Harold and Hatrack. That's nice." Then turning to the birds she greeted them enthusiastically. "Come to grandma." She swept the birds to her breast.

Mother never could differentiate between the two and called Pedro "Harold" and Pedra "Hatrack", then switched names so at the end of the first day even we did not know who they were.

Names did not matter since both quail accepted her with open beaks. She purchased starter mash, fresh oyster shell and even donated clusters of her prized dry-weed arrangements for snacks. They followed her in short rapid spurts about the house because she bribed them with a trail of cookies, bread crumbs and fresh broccoli.

Neighbors said mother's hobbies were her family, gardening and talking. They were wrong. It was her life. Early on she acquired the neighborhood talking-championship and sixty years later fiercely defended that title. In later times she honed her telephone technique and conversed hours without pause. Now she transferred that wondrous accomplishment to the birds. In fairness, they chatted too, for silence did not fit them. Mother loved it.

"Those birds sure can talk," she said. "I think Hatrack's better than the other one." So the trio followed each other, the quail flying to her lap when she sat. Apparently, they had much in common. Watching them though her magnifying glass, they passed happy hours together.

Days quickly vanished and on a hot afternoon I strolled through mother's garden among tomatoes and fresh corn, thinking sentimentally about Pedro, who was perched contentedly in my arms. In a remarkably short period we had become great friends and though Betsi loved both birds, I owned Pedro. Yanking an ear of corn from the stalk, I shucked it and offered him milky kernels. He ate greedily, casting bright thankful eyes as we walked.

We had watched mother's growing affection for the birds. She had recently buried her last brother and remained the sole survivor in a family of nine. Not only had her family died, but most of her friends. One by one they dropped away leaving mom with her small home, her garden and her Yankees. And the Yankees had not been winning too regularly. Almost instantly the growing chicks seemed to fill that void. She visited with them constantly. They in turn adored her. Both birds shadowed her as she limped about the house, shifting dust and preparing pie crusts, for she was a champion pie-maker. As our departure date neared, we wondered how we could separate the three.

Both chicks had grown enormously since coming to Billings. Brown and white feathers covered teen-aged bodies and their oversized feet continued expanding. Muscle strength magnified surprisingly. Occasionally they squeezed from our hands and nearly escaped. We were in no need of mother's warning that both birds wanted complete freedom. No longer could we hold them in a single fist, now we needed both hands for each bird.

Most of all they enjoyed mother's home for, inside, they delighted in complete freedom. She insisted on full liberty and they flew unrestrained about her small rooms. Instinctively they gravitated around her and she voiced unconvincingly, high-pitched protests about their attention. One morning Pedra circled the living room twice and, in an abrupt flurry, landed on mother's head. She waved her arms in defense and the other quail flew to her moving hand. "That Harold really can fly," she cracked, "and knows how to pick landing strips."

Harold certainly could fly, whether he was Pedra or Pedro. So could Hatrack. They no longer were babies.

The birds seldom left mother during the day and one evening Harold and Hatrack sat on her shoulder in the comfortable living room listening to TV news and waiting for Yankee baseball scores. Family photographs filled an entire wall spilling across windows and behind curtains. Between the knotty-pine frames she had thrust recent snapshots so the wall presented an interesting, if non-chronological, pictorial history of her three-generation family. Doilies in appropriate sizes covered all furniture and mother sat contentedly under a parchment-shaded lamp.

We silenced the loud television after the Yankee scores were announced and mother nodded happily although the Yanks had split. "They're coming along fine." She smiled at Pedra. "You don't have to worry about those Yankees, son," she said to Hatrack. Mother never worried about gender either.

Satisfied, she leaned back in the overstuffed chair. I coughed in surprise. In profile and under the incandescent lamp she too appeared bird-like, the quail on her shoulder miniature images. I blinked, rubbing my eyes in disbelief at the uncanny image. In my eyes three quail rested in mother's chair.

A llama-wool afghan covered her hands and lap, for her bones were always chilled no matter the temperature. She meditated briefly and her eyes sparkled more brilliantly than usual. In the sudden absence of racket following the baseball scores mother raised her voice so she could hear herself. "I could take the quail," she shouted.

"What?" Betsi answered almost as loudly as though she had not heard correctly. Mother's blunderbuss demand, seriously thwarted by Betsi's quick reply, caused her to pause. When she continued it seemed as if she had thought about her statement for a generation or so. Her words came slowly but loudly. "I said I could keep Harold and What's-his-name here. I have more room than you."

Betsi closed her eyes as if to blot out mother's request and massaged her torn ligaments gently. Her words, too, came slowly and nearly in a whisper. "We're not going to keep them. We're going to take them back to Sun City and turn them loose."

Mother seemed a little more shriveled and her arthritic hands curled around the afghan, rolling it into tight knots. "You could turn them loose right here in my yard. I can take care of Harold and that other one."

Betsi's refusal, based on love for the growing birds, flowed from her heart. I understood. I didn't want to relinquish the birds either, especially Pedro. But mother did not capitulate easily. "What are you going to do when they mature?"

"Mature?"

"Yes, mature," mother replied glancing at the birds on her shoulder. Both quail had quieted and seemed neutral to the conversation, but Pedra, ever the trouble-maker, supported mother with subliminal coos.

Betsi shuddered as if she had been doused with ice water. "Like mate?"

"That's it," mother said and both birds fluttered to her head.

"I've never thought about it," Betsi confessed. "I never thought our babies would do things like that."

Mother snickered. "That ancient custom has survived. How many chicks do they have?"

Betsi sighed. "About twelve....more or less. It all depends." She seemed untracked with the new problem and mother did not hesitate.

"That makes fourteen including Harold and Hatrack. Is your home big enough?"

"Our yard isn't big enough for fourteen quail."

Mother glanced at me with the slyness of the very old. "I thought so. I'll be happy to adopt them now and you can take pick of the litter next year."

Betsi's stubbornness, supported by extra rations of maternal love, surfaced quickly. "No, we're not giving them away, even temporarily. I know they'd be happy here," (the birds standing on one leg atop mother's head seemed to agree) "but we'll find a way to take them home." Then seeing mother's dejection her confidence faded and Betsi whispered to herself, "Somehow we'll find a way."

Mother rubbed her eyes. "I understand. Next year you can bring me a pair. By that time there'll be babies for me." Apparently realizing their future had been decided, both birds drifted to mother's lap and stood, looking up at her with sympathetic eyes.

Betsi and I searched the room for a more satisfactory solution, but found none. We could not deny the love affair between mother and the quail. Her two-acre home, filled with fruit and shade trees provided an ideal place for all birds and animals. Also, our birds had fallen inexorably under her spell. Finally, Betsi blew her nose and cleared her throat. "We'll think about it tonight," she told mother.

That last evening Pedro and I wandered into the garden together. He seemed quieter than usual inside his sock. The hot dry night smelled of corn pollen floating over raspberry bushes. Recent plantings of cabbage and broccoli muddied with irrigation water, blocked my path. Mother's touch lay everywhere and I smiled at two recently-dug potato hills. She could never wait for their maturity, but plucked the small immature marbles from the earth and combined them with fresh green peas, often for breakfast. I reflected that her paradise was dimming and soon she would not walk here, listen to Yankee ball games or vote Republican. Maybe, I thought, we should leave the quail with her during the final years as sort of frosting on her cake.

Raspberry season had ended and only a few isolated ripe berries remained, but I probed through briars since Pedro had shown a fondness for them. I discovered one and offered him the berry. Safe in his sock, he plunged his tiny beak into the snack in rapid sharp thrusts. He stopped suddenly and glanced at me as though a thought occurred to him. He did not continue eating but stared up as though waiting for my reply.

"No," I found myself saying, "you're going back to Arizona with us. I won't leave you here, Pedro. Understand? I won't leave you." Then I glanced about, embarrassed that someone might be listening, but we were alone. Pedro, apparently satisfied, pecked again into his raspberry.

Mother kissed us goodbye next morning. She did not mention the birds, but I leaned from the camper window and spoke, "Sorry we couldn't leave the quail with you mother. We'll bring you a pair next year."

Mother accepted the information philosophically. "I've lived eighty-six years without quail on my head and shoulders. I can get along another eighty-six." She kicked dirt with her cane and continued. "You know what kids say today, 'Win some lose some.' That's the way it goes." She brushed a small tear away quickly as though swatting a gnat and shouted into the camper, "Goodbye Harold, goodbye, Hatrack. Come back and see me. Grandma'll be waiting."

As we backed away she flashed a slow, sad smile and tottered toward a bower of petunias, then turned and waved broad goodbyes with her diamond willow cane. 🐦

Chapter Six

The Crazy Mountains stretched westward. The Yellowstone Valley, bisected by old Highway 10, lazied in a golden haze of ripened wheat. Cattle sought shade under broad cottonwood groves and a bald eagle—for eagles regularly fished the Yellowstone River—soared as a speck above shimmering valley heat. Although still on crutches, Betsi's soreness had faded and in exceptional good humor we hummed off-key ballads and, driving away from the morning sun, basked in pleasant childhood memories.

Our quail, imprisoned behind us in the apple box, neither remembered pleasant memories nor acquired any during the day. Ten days with mother's free-wheeling attitude whetted their appetites for expanded freedom. They protested continuously and mounted savage sorties against the mosquito netting. By nightfall they had destroyed all the feathers atop their heads and in profile resembled small, angry vultures.

Travelling normally calmed the birds, but all day long they tumbled about with a chip on their wings. In camp, they spent an hour angrily pacing around the wire enclosure. Worms and fresh broccoli, although grudgingly accepted, did nothing to change their disposition. A bee was trapped in their bonnet and they protested mightily against prison life.

Betsi dragged a rotten willow stump charged with ant larvae to their cage. They savagely destroyed it more out of pettiness than satisfied dining. Once, in the act of devouring three ants, Pedra suddenly stopped and leaped to the netting in protest and a patch of blood oozed from her skinned head. So obvious was her desire for freedom that we regretted not leaving both birds with mother. A sensible person had rolled a jackpine stump near the fire and we sat together, leaning against it, seriously talking about returning to Billings. In the end we compromised. If we discovered a covey of quail within our mountain camps we would free them instantly.

43

Every campground owns a distinct personality and Mill Creek Camp in the Tobacco Root mountains quickly revealed its special brand. It all started when a Lewis and Clark expedition scout wandered into the rugged valley and discovered a root he could dry and smoke, thus naming the entire range after his nicotine fix. We discovered other surprises.

Where else would one find tomato-eating butterflies, courting horned owls or watch W.C. Fields' nose drop into the campfire? And that didn't count the lady who harbored termites in her arteries. Such a camp could provide a receptive quail family looking for the Arizona royal blood of Pedro and Pedra.

The weird camping episode actually began when a miniature garden spider joined us, uninvited, at a filling station in Sheridan, Montana. She staked squatter's rights above the sun visor on Betsi's side of the camper. We normally did not accept hitch hikers but the photogenic spider seemed docile enough and if she wanted a ride into the Tobacco Roots, we agreed to furnish a one-way trip. Jostling along the gravel road the spider began weaving a web from the visor to the window wing. The exceedingly bumpy road demanded full driving attention, but between chuck holes and horseshoe curves, I sneaked glances at the insect who was determined to build its castle in our camper. Betsi maintained a running verbal account of the success-failure rate each time the spider swung, pendulum fashion, from the sunscreen to the window. By the time we reached Mill Creek camp, she had completed her basic web.

Neither of us is a great spider lover and we decided our transient friend had over impinged on our hospitality. When Betsi opened the door the web stretched, tightened and snapped. The black and red spider scurried across the visor and peered downward while Betsi eliminated web remnants from the corner in one devastating sweep. The spider did not appear disturbed and when Betsi offered her (we believed the hitch hiker to be a mother) a small cardboard carpet, she quickly stepped on it and Betsi transferred her to the nearest Douglas fir. She settled inside its craggy bark and rested. We thought no more of her until the following morning when we discovered she had again entered the camper and built another web, this time a beautifully designed home, in the identical area on the right wing window. Apparently she had

44

worked most of the night trying to impress us with her homesteading talent and interest in cross country travel. After a brief discussion, we extended her lease and decided to carry her with us when we left the Tobacco Roots.

At dusk butterflies came to us like homing pigeons. We had never attracted such quiet visitors and it was tomatoes that did it. During season our table offered tomatoes twice daily and it was not unusual to chomp into the garden-ripe fruit for breakfast. Betsi ate plain tomato sandwiches or, as she explained, bread sandwiches with a slice of tomato. I enjoyed thick juicy slices most of all with a sprinkle of salt, not diluted with bread, bacon or lettuce. Only tomatoes. So did the butterflies.

Earlier we had purchased ten pounds of freshly picked fist-sized tomatoes and I was cutting stem-ends from them when the first butterfly arrived. He was a monarch. The multicolored insect coasted to a landing strip on the tomato, dropped his drinking tube and sucked. Hot weather beer drinkers never seemed thirstier. Then he rested a moment or two, ignoring my tomato knife, and drank deeply again. Finally, thirst satisfied, he raised his head and seemed to nod to me in thanks, then fluttered away. He was not the only winged visitor that evening.

I called Betsi when three smaller, lavender butterflies arrived at the tomato table. Without waiting for invitations they invaded the juicy slices and quenched their thirst. Half a dozen others came and drank before flying away. I watched in amazement having never seen such a singular phenomenon. Neither had Betsi. Several water sources were readily available to them. Why did they choose tomatoes? How did they find our fruit? Had they ever drunk fresh tomato juice before? We never learned answers and butterflies never drank at our tomato trough again.

The soft-spoken evening darkened. Not far away on the north side of the valley a horned owl called. Seconds later, south of the valley and a mile or two distant, a female answered. He hooted a melancholy reply, but she did not answer. "She's flying to him," Betsi romanticized as the second owl remained quiet. Again the male hooted long, confidential invitations. No reply. Then he lowered his voice, seemingly looking directly into her eyes and hooting low, insistent whispers into the darkened mountains. It was a night for romance. No echoes followed but within a minute two contented hoots, close together, reached us and conversation continued among the pines. Betsi snuggled against me. "I wish you would court me like that," she said tossing broccoli remnants into the quail cage.

We had noticed another person in the near-empty camp earlier, but owls, campfires and butterflies occupied our attention so we were surprised when a shuffle of pine needles announced our next visitor. She was a large woman draped in a camouflage poncho (although we had not seen rain the entire trip), a red bandana harnessed her long black hair and her lips puckered in a tight line. She appeared to be on the unhappy side of fifty and broad sorrow creases, accentuated by firelight, lined her face. I poked the fire and cried our usual greeting, "Welcome to our camp. How are you?"

"Sick," she answered, "sick."

Florence Nightingale Betsi looked up from the quail cage. "Can we help?"

"No," the woman said, "I'm dying."

"Oh!" Betsi cried quickly deciding this case lay beyond her aspirin-milk of magnesia medical kit. "What's the matter?"

"Termites," the woman announced, "termites in my blood. You ain't had pain till you got termites."

"Goodness," Betsi moaned for lack of other sympathy as the woman continued.

"How I suffer," she said in low, convincing tones, "they been crawling in my blood six months. Clear up to my fingertips." She lifted her arms and spread her stubby fingers for inspection. Backlit against dancing firelight I thought I could see a stream of something coursing through her veins but did not identify termites.

"My heart beats all the time with these termites," she told us. "All the time!"

"My God!" Betsi marvelled. "What can doctors do for you?"

"They give me protozoan," she said earnestly. "I wouldn't be alive today without it. I am a special case."

"I believe that," I told her and Betsi kicked me sharply for she could not tolerate agony.

"Protozoan helped. I still have termites and I suffer. How I suffer! But I'm alive. Thank God for protozoan." She paused and looked into the cage. "You got a bird," she said. "What kind?"

"Two birds," Betsi replied tossing the remaining broccoli through the cage and watching Pedra and Pedro leap at their dessert. "They're Gambel's quail."

"Like I said," the woman continued hardly glancing at the hopping birds, "I suffer death with them termites, but I take protozoan three times a day and here I am." She waddled into darkened snowberry bushes beneath the pines and disappeared from our lives.

"I need a chocolate bar." Betsi spoke to the quail. "I'm suffering too."

We assumed Mill Creek Camp had doled enough excitement for that evening, but we were wrong. The climax came later. The campground provided a bonanza of firewood and we took full advantage of the bounty. Flames leaped high as we tucked the quail inside their bags and we four sat flushed with heat and contentment. As usual, after dark the birds seemed tired and ready for the apple box, yet reluctant to retire. Their heads darted toward the fire, upward through pine boughs and then quizzically at us as if they wanted a bedtime story. Unknown to them the story unfolded within the embers.

The spitting heat crested and a combination of pitch and moisture produced startling snorts and explosions in the ring of fire. When embers displaced flames we began a favorite game...discovering people or events in the glowing mass. We did not wait long.

A crippled Spanish galleon, fully aflame, materialized along the far fringe of coals and burned brightly a few seconds then exploded and sank into a glowing grave. We leaned forward with excitement when a fiery dragon nearly three feet long sprang from the fire box and spit flames into the night. She died abruptly when her neck collapsed and dropped into the disappearing hulk of the galleon, her tail still waving in splendid fury. We had barely settled back into our camp chairs when along the heated border a portrait of W. C. Fields glowed. His image was unmistakable and we both agreed it was Bill although the quail did not comment. For nearly a moment—longer than most fire sculptures—W. C. Fields' suspicious eyes watched us with his churlish smirk, then with a quick snap his bulbous nose separated and fell over his chin. So vivid had his portrait been we almost heard him say "Drat!" as his lips collapsed in fiery protest.

With the fire nearly spent, we rose to bed the quail, but suddenly Betsi pointed a finger. "There's Moses," she cried and both quail stared wide-eyed at her unexpected scream. "Couldn't be," I disagreed. "His nose is too long and I don't see the commandments. Anyhow it can't be Moses...it's Jesus. Jesus on the cross!!" With dramatic clarity we watched the Savior stretched over a cross of coals more clearly than all other images. Silently his arms dropped, his head broke with a characteristic hangman's snap and the cross beneath him crumbled. The show over, both quail slept in our arms unaffected by the dramatic finale, for they were not especially religious. They preferred broccoli and meal worms to parables and barely moved when we placed them in the apple box. Returning to the bed of coals, we drenched the fire with buckets of mountain water and a predictable hissing steam cloud rose above us.

"It's Old Faithful," I told Betsi. "Yes," she replied, "Old Faithful in winter...let's go to bed. I'm tired."

At breakfast next morning the quail, in sleeping bags, were eating cream of wheat at the table when Betsi suddenly sprang up. "Our spider!" she cried. "She might be hungry too." Betsi hobbled quickly to the camper on a single crutch and brought the sleepy spider to our table. "Breakfast time!" she said to the spider, but Pedra thought Betsi spoke to her and quickly pecked at the colorful insect. Before we could interfere, she swallowed the spider and chomped several more times as though smacking her beak. Betsi stared in astonishment. "It's my fault," she said, "I didn't know she liked spiders for breakfast."

We searched,too, for the dying lady with termites in her blood, but she had departed. We never saw her again. We would have searched the obituaries but we never learned her name and our curiosity remained unanswered.

Better times lay ahead at Liberty Lake, Washington, our next stop. There, Betsi's brother owned a lake shore condominium with breathing space, verdant landscaping and a leash law. We prayed the lake might prove a halfway house between camping and complete freedom for the quail.

Next day chocoholic Betsi entered heaven at Liberty Lake for her sister-in-law, Jacquie, also a self-confessed addict, welcomed a sister sinner. While they retired to a glut of brownies, fudge and chocolate mousse, Arnie and I settled for beer and steak. We abandoned shoes and stretched legs over the lanai railing, recalling often-told lies. Quickly we settled into a world of calories and laughter. Even the quail thrived for they cherished fresh lawn as a cage floor and moved with us to the lanai each evening. They bedded, quite happily, in the apple box after sundown and it appeared they had forgotten the joys of magnificent freedom in Billings.

Days and nights vanished quickly with our favorite in-laws and we faced the inevitable departure. The last evening we boated along the lake shore at dusk, mocking kildeer and hooting at owls. Daylight left reluctantly. The quail beside us in their sleeping bags seemed more relaxed and contented than usual. We docked and clambered through a buttercup field up the sloping lawn to prepare bedtime for the birds. Canada lay ahead. Our visit, as usual, had been nearly perfect.

In preparation for road travel Betsi had washed the feather duster, for the birds no longer slept in bags on mild summer nights. They much preferred the comparative freedom and comfort of the fluffy feathers. New gravel and sand inside the apple box smelled fresh and inviting and, as added protection against ever-increasing strength of the quail, Betsi stretched new strong netting over the top.

We shared bedding responsibilities. The quail's substantial teen-age strength grew daily and we no longer attempted to manage them alone. I secured Pedra while Betsi cuddled Pedro for last minute prayers. He liked to retire first and she held him, whispering soft mother-talk in his ear. Unpinning a small corner in the box she aimed him, as always, into the opening when suddenly, without warning he sprang from her hands, backed through the open vent and fluttered to Jacquie and Arnie's garage roof. With a desperate plunge Betsi discarded her crutch and instinctively leaped after him but, lacking wings, grasped only thin Liberty Lake air.

The formality of freedom staggered Pedro momentarily and he balanced precariously on a gnarled cottonwood limb towering above us. His head tipped on one side and he regarded us as strangers. He did not wait long. Carried by a soft evening breeze and instinct far more powerful than warmth, security—and my friendship—Pedro sprang into the darkened branches and disappeared.

A second or two lapsed before our minds cleared. It was one of those moments that can be remembered, examined and analyzed in minute detail during odd hours in a lifetime. Then the enormity of our loss struck us like thunder. Urgently we called again and again. A brief flicker of hope came when we watched a shadow move toward us through the foliage of the blackening cottonwood. It proved to be a curious young sapsucker and he flew upward and out of sight. Stars brightened, the sky grew dark, and against the dimming of light the cottonwood merged into the sky and disappeared. As it vanished, our hopes for Pedro's return faded too.

We climbed atop the garage and called repeatedly. Usually the quail answered, but only Pedra replied softly. Lonely and secure under her feather duster, she seemed as depressed as we. A light rain of cotton catkins drifted down and a loon called among rushes along the lake shore. Betsi exhaled deeply several times and grasped my hand firmly for comfort. Finally she spoke. "He's free. That's what he wanted. That's what we wanted." Then the dam broke and she cried for her lost friend.

We waded through the dark side of the moon and morning finally came. Pedro's food can, left outside as enticement, stood untouched during the long night. We reclimbed the garage among crusty cottonwood branches and cried into its leaves and branches. He did not answer. "He's not here," I finally admitted. "He's gone."

There was a pause and I could feel my heart beating. "I know," she cried, dividing her slice of misery with me.

We never saw him again.

Deep agony enveloped us as we packed. Pedro's disastrous escape clouded our minds and we muddled Pedra's future. Betsi bent over the apple box and stared at the quiet little bird who seemed suddenly older and deep in thought. Finally Betsi spoke. "They've been together from the beginning. Let's not separate them now."

"After breakfast," I said.

But our appetites had disappeared along with Pedro so we walked to Pedra's box. Betsi stripped the clothespins away and uncovered the top. The teen-aged quail crouched desolately under the colorful duster peeking up at us sideways as if asking what had happened to her brother. Her food lay untouched.

"Don't change your mind," I said. "Let her go."

"I won't change," Betsi said firmly. She reached into the box and lifted Pedra slowly into the air unfolding her palm as her hand elevated. Pedra rested snugly in her hand and, all barriers gone, sat uncertainly, nodding at freedom in the cottonwood. "Go! Go find your brother," Betsi commanded and jiggled her hand a bit.

Pedra half turned, stared at us then trotted down Betsi's arm, rested lightly on her shoulder and peeped into her ear. She stood balanced on one foot staring at us for help. Then, displaying further evidence of her decision, she folded her legs and snuggled tightly against Betsi's neck as if nesting. Tears, again, splashed Betsi's cheeks and she turned to us questioningly.

Arnie spoke first. "She'll die if she stays. Winters here are too hard for Gambel's. You've lost one. If you want the other, take her." Jacquie's ringside seat at our loss had not been easy and she nodded agreement.

The pain of tears quieted Betsi's heart a bit and her hand crept to her neck and fondled young Pedra. Without protest Pedra hopped into the open apple box and dodged in her feathery hideaway. Betsi pinned the netting.

Liberty Lake seemed cold and sinister and the tires spit gravel on the cottonwood tree as we backed away, steering toward Osoyoos, British Columbia, three camping days distant. We never looked back, for Betsi's pale face echoed my heart. Words of sympathy seemed meaningless so we remained silent.

The crisis of misfortune followed us like a sad dog and our day of wretchedness dragged on. The VW, always dependable, lagged along the lodgepole-fringed road and rewarded us with a flat tire in the rain. It seemed much colder and Pedra huddled quietly under her duster, offering neither consolation nor explanation for her brother's defection.

Toward evening enemy clouds moved over us. They tumbled around black as tar until ear-splitting thunder finally cracked through the van. Even anticipating the barrage I shuddered and leaped in the seat, clasping the steering wheel ever tighter while lightning enveloped us. The earth seemed on fire. Whopping acetylene torch-like flames, sharp and blue, touched forest greenery in crisp fiery bursts. The pattern never varied. Each streak jabbed the earth and an instant of blackness followed, then explosive thunder roared from the point of impact as a burst of flame exploded through the rain and we watched the birth of another forest fire. The world would learn tomorrow that nine fires still burned sixteen miles along the highway. We steered inside the vortex as the storm whirled around us threatening, thundering and chopping slashes of yellow-blue flame into the wet forest.

I could see no road, only splashes of blinding rain, and in frustration coasted to a stop, praying a massive trailer would not rear-end us. Betsi and I had long discovered the value of silence in similar situations and Pedra also remained mute, shrinking ever smaller within the sock, blinking her eyes at the swinging wipers.

Bottled violence survives only so long and the gut-busting cloudburst finally raced up the valley, dissolving into low grumbling rolls. A faint, luminous glow trailed through the rain curtain. We splashed down the highway weary and depressed, dodging watery tidal waves following passage of every loaded lumber truck. Betsi spotted a National Forest campground and we drove inside.

It was no night for champagne. Even steaming cups of strong camp tea failed to revive our spirits and we sat, heads bowed, around the damp smoky fire. Betsi flung a fistful of pine cones into the embers and as exploding flames framed her tightly clamped jaw, she muttered, "I suppose Canadian customs will confiscate Pedra in Osoyoos. She'll be an illegal alien, you know."

I knew! In an effort to ease the problem I said, "No. We'll go home first. The mounties won't take Pedra."

Somewhere in darkness a predatory coyote howled and, thinking of Pedro, it was a sound I preferred not to hear. Suddenly gripping a thick juniper branch I attacked the campfire as though the smoke, embers and half-burned logs were responsible for losing my bird. As the sputtering fire died I knew it wasn't any of those factors. It was the call of the wild. ◥

52

Chapter Seven

A string of untidy dreams plagued Betsi throughout the night and she kicked me within the double sleeping bag, muttering unhappy moans and grunts. Next morning she comforted Pedra, cocooned in the woolen sock, on her lap and they rested silently together contemplating the yellow-striped highway, listening to Johnny Cash songs. Pedra from time to time lifted her head and peered through the sweeping windshield wiper, cooing softly.

I drove, hands firmly fixed on the wheel, trying to cope with bad luck and worse weather. Uncertain of our future I grappled with the thought of returning to Arizona. Even the VW seemed reluctant to continue, coughing and sputtering asthmatically in the rain. We splashed down the road until nightfall and camped in a drizzling forest, contemplating next day's border crossing.

Smuggling is always a problem especially if one is an amateur. We had previously bootlegged eight fresh papaya seeds (Betsi wanted a papaya tree in her living room) through the Hawaiian agriculture station but that experience scarcely qualified us as experts. We felt especially unqualified to smuggle an unregistered wild bird through suspicious Mounties and suffered nerve-tearing guilt complexes while driving north. Yet we wanted to travel in Canada. A trembling fever overcame Betsi that night and she lay without sleep listening to Pedra's quiet monologues.

Around midnight Pedra stirred in bed, then uttered a terrified nightmarish scream. Betsi crawled to the box and calmed her bird, but it was false counseling for it was Betsi who needed confidence—and I. Not Pedra.

In darkness she whispered, "They'll take her. I know the Mounties will take her," in what was a rare admission of defeat. Then folding herself close to me she suggested, "Let's go home." I feigned deafness, not daring a midnight decision.

Fretful damp clouds surrounding us drifted south during the night and dawn broke in spectacular splendor. The sun pierced through towering Douglas firs and a warm autumn breeze shook prisms of sparkling rain drops on us as a dog shakes water. But the sun shone! Wet weather, it appeared, had vanished.

I puzzled which direction to aim the camper, but when Betsi finished breakfast, she said, "What are we waiting for? Let's go to Canada." Then she broke into laughter, wildly elated that we had not allowed a tragic loss and a three-day rain storm spoil our trip. "To hell with the Mounties, to hell with Customs. Canada, here we come!" she sang, her fist high in the air. Pedra raised her head in astonishment. Fifteen minutes later we were on the road.

A good deal of her sparkle dimmed by the time we saw the border station. "Let's ask somebody who knows about these things." She pointed an authoritative finger toward a gasoline station.

As we drove into the station two attendants intently inspected a scandal tabloid in their hands. Screaming headlines declared, with blurred photographs, a gorilla and native girl's intimate involvement and the resultant offspring. We claimed little knowledge in that area and listened, as eavesdroppers, open-mouthed. Apparently even the caste system had been violated, for the girl was the daughter of a local chieftain. Reluctantly Betsi coughed loudly, pointed to one of the men and told him her problem.

The long-haired skinny fugitive from a barber stared as though he understood. Red-spiked whiskers blended unevenly into a blotchy complexion and his wrap-around hair style only accentuated premature baldness. He spoke with a slight lisp through his wispy moustache and raised his arms displaying copper amulets on both wrists. "Hell, lady, they ain't gonna ass you no questions you don't ass them none. No sweat. Don't say nothin'. Unnastand?" Betsi nodded. He rang up the gasoline charge and returned to his study on gorilla fertility rites.

"I know what to do now," Betsi said confidently and tucked a startled half-grown quail into her blouse.

"You can't do that. There isn't room," I argued.

Betsi smiled hugging herself through the blue parka, partly to protect against the damp morning chill and partly to hide Pedra stashed inside her bosom. "When we get to the border jes don' say nothin' they don' ass you," she advised. "Unnastand?" She seemed extremely proud, confident and self-satisfied.

The starched Royal Mountie appeared as official as anyone I'd ever seen when we drove under the sheltered station. He also looked liked a hybrid Robert Redford-Burt Reynolds, Betsi told me later. "Any guns, fruit or liquor?" he queried.

"None."

"How long will you be in Canada?"

"Ten days."

"Have a good trip," he smiled warmly and waved good-bye.

Pedra clucked quietly inside Betsi's blouse and blinked as though emerging from a darkened tunnel when Betsi finally unzipped her parka. Betsi was ecstatic. Her eyes opened wide as they usually did when she was happy and she patted my knee with firm victorious thumps. She carried Pedra to her lap like a prize and cuddled her gently again and again. The pair began conversing non-stop.

At dinnertime two champagne glasses and a green Christmas candle decorated the camp table, which was unusual because it was September and we did not drink champagne. Betsi spooned red pepper jelly and cream cheese on crisp crackers and, coals ready, I roasted thick steaks over cedar coals—Betsi's extra well done and mine rare. Pedra seemed relaxed and contented as embers faded inside the fire ring and a new moon ploughed through fields of tumbling clouds. If Pedra suffered another nightmare or Betsi moaned in darkness I did not know, for I slept as if drugged.

Without her brother Pedra transformed, almost over-night, into a different personality. The formerly churlish, testy, chick accepted, with less protest, our selection of campsites and food, but most of all, she chatted constantly with Betsi as a trusted friend. The pair never lacked conver-sational material and Pedra always accompanied us on sidetrips tucked inside her sock, peering, reporting and radiating happiness.

She apparently enjoyed Canadian scenery and relished the Okanogan bumper fruit crop and, we thought, seemed eager when we again crossed the border and boarded the Anacortes, Washington, ferry for the San Juan Islands.

55

Orcas Island, our favorite among the San Juans, welcomed us with bright sun and we set camp in the shade of Constitution Mountain along Cascade Lake. Coarse gray sand and a whiff of ocean blended pleasantly with ponderosa pine and wild gentian. Narrow blacktopped roads curved around the horseshoe shaped island to Deer Harbor, Doe Bay and Eastsound. We discovered Olga later. Quiet ripples lapped at our toes a few feet from camp, decorating the sand with frail, white spittle swirls. Within minutes visitors joined us.

No camper has ever forgotten rabbits on Orcas Island. Thousands of rabbits. Tens of thousands! Through some sort of rabbit grapevine they divided campers among them. Our quota, apparently, was four. The plump, shiny animals established squatters rights instantly and sniffed at our table before we sat down. Quiet and inoffensive, they accepted food as a reward for companionship. We thought them charming.

Our bird did not. Although the rabbits introduced themselves on the spot, Pedra hated them instantly. The rabbits did not mind. Only the wire barricade prevented them from shaking hands with her. Sniffing and nibbling grass around the pen's edge, they shot inquiring glances at the strange fluttering foreigner inside, even stretching over the cage to obtain a better view. Pedra fretted and backed away when they continued fraternizing, her black serpent eyes darting to us in a plea for help. Betsi removed her from the pen the first day and called the friendly bunnies to meet their travelling cousin. She thought a face-to-face introduction might abolish apprehension. The four bunnies came willingly and squatted in a circle eager to play, but Pedra buried herself in Betsi's hands and refused to visit. She remained aloof and skeptical, finally accepting them only as necessary nuisances.

But she liked nearly all others. One exception wandered into camp a sunny afternoon leaning heavily on his brass-headed cane and smelling strongly of wintergreen. His clothes did not label him a camper, for he wore a heavy tweed jacket and a gaily colored yellow scarf around his throat. Nibbling his gray moustache (Betsi claimed he nibbled more effectively than the rabbits) he ignored us, sucked his teeth and paused in front of Pedra's pen.

As he stopped, a rabbit leaped on his leg in friendliness. The man's cane stabbed firmly into the rabbit's ribs and the gentle animal retreated six inches, then stared with puzzled wonderment at the man.

"Go!" the Englishman commanded, his moustache twitching. The rabbit reared on his hind legs in a begging position, but the Englishman ignored it. Instead, he retrieved a pair of steel-rimmed spectacles from his jacket and perched them on his ruddy nose, squinting at Pedra. The glasses wobbled as he bent and he appeared to look over, rather than through the thick lenses. His cane punched the earth directly in front, touching the cage, and he teetered back on his heels. "Haw," he grunted as though speaking through a dirty sock.

Pedra glanced at him sideways and issued a cacophony of insults. The Englishman rocked back and forth a few times and digested Pedra's information, then reopened his mouth. "Ah." The word filtered through his moustache. "I say. Ah." A slight breeze shifted the smell of his cologne so strongly that Pedra sneezed. She leaped into the air several times, fluttered her wings and retreated to the distant corner of the cage then stared with bewilderment. The man looked glum for a couple of seconds and mumbled, "I say." He paused thoughtfully and removed his spectacles, replaced them carefully in his jacket pocket, and stumped away. Subsequently the myopic word miser crossed camp several times. Without exception Pedra reacted violently to his presence. Did she dislike the man personally? Why? Did his moustache disturb her? We wondered if the Englishman disliked birds and manifested, in some manner, his hatred. We never knew. Pedra communicated, but she did not speak.

With the exception of the Englishman, her heart reached out to almost everyone in camp. She especially fascinated children. They tottered over, pointed stubby fingers into the cage and tried climbing inside. Pedra, at ease, chatted with them and enjoyed every minute. She ignored no child and they returned repeatedly with parents, grandparents and cameras. Because of Pedra, the charmer, our fleeting paths crossed—and touched—hundred of friends we might otherwise have missed.

She adored Nipper. He came to us one afternoon astride a massive red Hurricane Honda cycle, wearing a blue plastic helmet, black leather jacket, goggles and sporting a zest for life. The eleven-year-old wire-haired terrier had ridden cycles six years and called western Ontario home. He had been travelling nearly a month when his owners lifted him from his seat on the gasoline tank.

Age and arthritis slowed his progress and he stretched stiff-legged around the cycle a few times, urinated on a nearby tree and, catching Pedra's scent, stalked slowly toward her cage. Strangely, she did not appear frightened. The dog examined her carefully and Pedra, who had never seen a terrier garbed in goggles, helmet and jacket, stared back. Then they nuzzled at the cage. An instant aura of friendship bloomed under the ponderosa pine that afternoon and Nipper never left the area except at mealtime.

His owners appeared. Nipper-the-Icebreaker, they called him. He made more friends than they did. Still honeymooning after six years, the woman was undecided whether she loved her husband more than Nipper, who had come with the wedding ring. They disrobed him and he appeared as a normal old terrier, but still remained with Pedra. His action did not surprise the man. "Three years ago in Saskatchewan he fell in love with a pet desert tortoise," he told us. "They became inseparable. It was a weird match," he admitted, "because the tortoise didn't like Nipper at all. Simply stayed in his shell and refused to communicate."

We suspected an ulterior motive on Pedra's part. The bunnies remained a safe distance from the dog, and that alone was reason enough to accept his friendship. No matter, campers came with cameras to record the strange relationship and, when the trio drove away two days later (Nipper goggled and drenched with water for he became overheated during travel), we were surprised when a neighboring camper mentioned Nipper's owners being different, too. She was a Norwegian blonde and he an African black. Pedra had not noticed and neither had we.

Blackberrying at Olga gave us a ready excuse for morning outings and an excellent source for good food. The tiny coastal hamlet, bisecting a dirt crossroad 30 minutes from camp, provided thickets of plentiful wild blackberries. We loved them. Juicy and ripe and large as a woodman's thumb the berries quickly filled our bucket and we sang to the world-at-large in the blackberry brambles.

Pedra was always in excellent humor on blackberry hunts and watched from the camper, where we allowed her freedom within the locked vehicle. In thirty minutes we overfilled containers and drove back to camp. There we rinsed, baptized the berries with heavy cream and sugar, and prepared the feast.

On a whim we completely released Pedra because her mind, once fixed on food, never strayed. Discovering she would never desert a ripe banana, a plump strawberry or a freshly picked blackberry, all of us celebrated her limited freedom at the table. We filled three blackberry bowls. Pedra raced to her bowl like a homing pigeon, plunged into the dish nearly burying her head and savored the prime berries. She then briefly glanced at us as though saying, "This is delectable," thereby breaking one of her conversational rules for she normally spoke only in monosyllables. In her excitement she fixed a solid foot on her dish then shoveled in berries as though she had just finished an extensive fast. After a few gluttonous pecks, she raced to our bowls and wolfed berries under our noses glancing at us guiltily as though she had been caught with her beak in the cookie jar.

Pedra's improbable relationship with me relaxed as days flew by. She tolerated me, along with the rabbits, as a necessary nuisance. Our conversations displayed none of the animation she enjoyed with Betsi, her confidant. In spite of an aloof spirit, more and more I thought of Pedra with tenderness and caught myself smiling at things she did. It especially pleased me when she stole my blackberries. I relished her saucy morning chatter and happy acceptance of bed at night. Chuckling aloud at her cavalier attitude toward the Englishman, I began to realize she was more of an asset to camping life than I ever imagined. Slowly my objections to Pedra vanished and we became silent partners.

But confinement milked Pedra's patience dry. Nearly two months old, she aggressively petitioned for additional freedom. Increasingly antagonistic toward the cardboard prison and wire cage, she repeatedly attacked the stout net above her. After several days her plume again disappeared and first glances suggested a feisty bald eagle in the cage.

"Adolescent rebellion," Betsi explained. "She wants more freedom."

"What'll we do?"

Betsi curled her upper lip and licked her fingers. She had just finished a Snickers bar and remnants of melted chocolate smudged her hands. She sat quietly licking them clean and thinking. She always thought better when under the influence of chocolate. "I'll think of something," she said.

Chapter Eight

The following morning Betsi overwhelmed herself with a miraculous idea. Her mind visualized a training harness for Pedra. With it the girls could walk together along the beach, through mountain trails and even—Betsi dreamed—into supermarkets. They would walk, hand-in-leash, in happy semirestricted freedom.

She drove to the Saturday Orcas flea market for needles, pins and velcro strips. I remained in camp, for Betsi possessed the ability to spend eight hours making a ten-second purchase. But I was wrong. She returned quickly, her fingers flew, and within an hour the harness lay on her lap completed. The marvelous contraption consisted of narrow padded straps adjusted to Pedra's breast and legs. Numerous fittings resulted in a tailored success, and in a fit of exuberance she kicked off her sandals and danced an Irish jig on the table. Only later did we realize she had not used crutches.

Pedra regarded the harness with an open mind. She tolerated the fittings without protest, for she was not a suspicious bird and probably thought it was just another of Betsi's transient ideas. How wrong she was. Betsi snipped the last thread with her teeth, breathed deeply, and borrowing a page from magicians who tranquilize birds by laying them on their backs, grasped little Pedra and rolled her over.

Pedra peeped quietly without enthusiasm, but did not resist the cinched straps around her feathers. Then, attaching a leash-type security cord to the harness, Betsi stood Pedra up in the sand. Pedra sucked in her breath, tightened her wings and tried to shimmy out of the straitjacket. A furious sparkle danced in her eyes and she skyrocketed upward in a spiral then fell down in a tangle. After catching her breath she chased the harness like a turpentined dog, but quickly became enmeshed in the cord and was doubly imprisoned. She failed, for the harness was Betsi-made and an emu would have been challenged to escape its coils. After

61

a series of Houdini contortions, Pedra sat down on her elbows and pecked furiously at the straps.

Betsi's smell of quick victory faded and I would not have given either side a chance for overwhelming success. But Betsi was determined. She stood over the little bird, untangled Pedra and said, "Come." I noticed the lines of her face harden. "We're going for a stroll." She tugged gently on the cord.

Pedra set her toes in the sand and looked at Betsi as though the wrong person occupied the straitjacket. Her pleading black eyes saw no mercy in Betsi's heart and she cocked her head in my direction, but my laughter turned her to the rabbits who scampered around the table in a display of neutrality. Betsi watched Pedra for a moment, softly humming a Kenny Rogers tune. It was a sign that I interpreted to be a danger signal. Then she pulled the line taut and stepped briskly forward. But Betsi had not reckoned on Pedra's tantalizing resistance for the tiny bird lay down shrieking and was dragged, feathers in the sand, her head flopping helplessly, the harness acting as a sort of a hangman's noose. Betsi stood bewildered in the path, defeated by the four-ounce quail at the end of her tether.

"Well," I said, realizing she had a task to sap her patience, "Pedra certainly doesn't act like a trained poodle."

She ignored me but her heart thundered in frustration. Turning, she set Pedra on her feet and muttered, "Come on!" and dangled her ahead like a suspended puppet. Pedra jerked along, her wings fluttering wildly, toes intermittently touching the sand and scratching erotic footprints that resembled a travelling egg beater.

Forty feet from camp the Englishman, cane in hand, emerged from his campsite. Immaculate in a fresh tweed jacket and paisley scarf he puffed his briar pipe and briskly approached the scene. Ten feet away he discovered Pedra struggling for freedom. Shoving his cane ahead as sort of a brake and not believing his eyes, he frantically searched for his glasses. A strained thin smile emerged through his moustache and, still sucking his pipe, he honked, "Haw!" Pedra stopped struggling, glanced at the man with an unwinking stare and screeched an obscenity at him. Her point made, she pivoted around and trotted back to camp almost pulling Betsi behind her.

Following the minor victory, Pedra's education progressed at such a snail's pace that Betsi watched clouds and dribbled sand through her fingers for hours on end. She dallied endless afternoons tracing abstract patterns in the sand wondering how to get her charge through the first grade. It was a case of stubbornness fighting stubbornness with plenty of ammunition on each side. I would not have wagered a nickel on either contestant.

Yet Betsi did not surrender. Every morning and every afternoon she harnessed Pedra and offered her the freedom of the leash. Pedra hated every meter. At the sight of the contraption she shrank as small as possible and, with imploring eyes and incoherent coos, pleaded Betsi not to subject her to another humiliating walk. But Betsi's improvisation was on the line. For her, the harness represented a marvelous dream and it would succeed. For Pedra it was a nightmare of scorpions, ghouls and death through humiliation.

Fortunately the rabbits enjoyed strolling as much as Pedra hated it. Always near our table, they could hardly wait for Pedra's educational hikes. They hopped along with Betsi and Pedra, quietly nibbling and enjoying the entire session. We never had better neighbors.

Betsi finally compromised. In view of Pedra's desperate pleas, Betsi decided to place her miraculous harness in cold storage. But only after a final walk together.

Late in the afternoon, on what was to be our final day at Orcas Island, the strange Englishman strolled quietly along a path directly in front of Pedra and Betsi. When they faced each other, he flicked his cane in greeting. Predictably Pedra exploded skyward, her flight feathers clawing the hated cord and, in midair raucously forbade the man to repeat the insult. She landed scarcely two feet from his big boots and cocked her head upward, turning her voice to full volume. Shouts, threats and quail invectives flowed uninteruptedly from the tiny warrior. The Englishman, a thousand times larger than she and armed with a cudgel, made no difference. Pedra had her say.

Admiration shone through the Englishman's glasses. He seemed delighted with her attention and anchored his cane more firmly into the ground, blocking the path. His searching eyes peered at the shrieking bird. Finally his tight lips made painful efforts to answer her volatile charges. When he actually spoke to Betsi, for the first time, she smiled despite her struggle to control Pedra's tantrum.

"Haw." He sucked through long stained teeth, "If you owned two of those youngsters they'd make a splendid team...difficult to break to harness, but splendid." Then plainly embarrassed at exposing his doubtful humor, he moved briskly toward the bathhouse, chortling to himself. "Haw," he honked hoarsely between giggles, "I say, haw!" And he disappeared into the spruce trees.

We never saw him again but upon returning from our moonlight stroll that evening Betsi spotted a wintergreen cologne box atop the table. It bore no message, but contained a generous supply of dry seed. Alongside, in a smaller gem box lay three plump luscious blackberries. Pedra had chalked up another convert.

She enjoyed campfires on Vancouver Island, ate crumpets and trifles in Victoria, B.C., then we carried her, encased in her mummy bag, above deck on the Black Ball ferry to watch Port Angeles appear in the mist.

Remarkably warm, dry weather followed us but we still cast anxious eyes at Hurricane Ridge in Olympic National Park. Fresh snow covered its crest and the next morning a diaphanous ice skein appeared in our wash basin. We recalled early Montana winters and headed south.

But, for us, Olympic National Park was a place for pleasant recollections. Happy ghosts appeared along the way and we settled a few days beneath Sitka spruce and mottled red-vine maples. Our hiking boots brushed fiddlehead ferns under moss-draped Douglas fir. We balanced like tightrope walkers atop great derelict driftwood skeletons on sunset beaches at La Push. The idyllic life set our anchors firmer than planned, for we thrived on an unprogrammed philosophy. Our hearts reached out to Pedra screaming for freedom. We understood.

To allow more freedom we secured her with a velcro leg-strap to small pieces of driftwood or a pinecone. She tugged an inch at a time about camp, pecking and scratching grass seed and casting pitiful glances at us as she struggled. Betsi's heart broke watching the little bird dragging a giant cone through snags of grass and weeds, but we could think of no other solution. It was leg chains or return to the mesh-wire prison!

In one camp she discovered large black ants and her ant disposal method seemed unusual. She attacked the sharp-biting insects with a fierce peck to the head then, after a series of energetic jerks at their body, quickly consumed the delicacy tail first. She never ate it otherwise. The huge ants must have been delicious for, after each ant disappeared, she gazed at us intently as if giving thanks, then hobbled forward in search of others.

Ant hunting was an educational facet both Betsi and Pedra enjoyed so the two hunted together in weeds and scrub brush with Betsi happily pointing out killer ants or brown beetles with her driftwood walking stick. She had discarded her crutches and shared limited freedom, too. Between hunts Pedra fluttered her wings in sudden bursts of enthusiasm. Other times she became hopelessly entangled in a snare of harness, cord, pinecones and grass. Lying helpless in her handmade web, she called pitiful cries and cast black glances at us as though we were responsible for her predicament. Her point was well made. She ranked freedom higher than three guaranteed meals. Her frantic desire for liberty strengthened our decision to release her the instant we returned to Sun City.

We decided to establish a half-way house inside the camper and completely free her, only covering her at night for protection. We feared she might join us in bed and suffer irreparable damage.

On the first day Pedra could not believe her good fortune. Waiting hesitantly within the open apple box Betsi called and tempted her with broccoli and sunflower seeds. She finally leaped to the box edge—teetered unbelievingly—and regarded us with a devilish grin, then puffed out her tiny breast and cooed rapid, rapturous messages. A short leap carried her to the refrigerator and onward to Betsi's shoulder, where she perched and nibbled on Betsi's ear.

After that she automatically came to the towel-draped dashboard as soon as Betsi released her. There she chatted, ate and preened. She slept contentedly on the dashboard without tumbling to the floor as we meandered down the coastline.

Pedra earned highest marks as a travelling companion. She never insisted on a coffee break, a shopping spree or a rest stop. She was always ready to go! Perched on Betsi's lap

munching sunflower seeds, her encouraging chatter short-
ened our travelling time. So, with Pedra atop the dashboard,
hours disappeared rapidly and days merged into a week of
happy zig-zagging along the Oregon coast. ➤

Chapter Nine

We hit California on a crisp, no-nonsense autumn morning that smelled of burned pinecones and mushrooms. Happy birds sang along barbed wire fences and optimism filled the air. The California Agriculture inspection station faced us promptly and we anticipated no problems. Canadian entries had been easy. Now, a stalwart female inspector challenged us cheerfully. "What's in the box?" she asked peeking into the packed camper.

"A quail," I answered without hesitation.

"California quail?" Her dark neatly plucked eyebrows lowered perceptibly. Her smile remained, but I decided I did not like her attitude.

"No, Gambel's," I said and noticed sweat on my palms. "It's a pet."

She frowned and her puckered brows swelled into wrinkles. "I don't think you can import Gambel's. There's some sort of regulation." The sparkle of her inspector's badge struck me in the eye and I winced when she stepped into her booth and grasped a telephone. We were trapped!

Quiet terror overwhelmed Betsi and she grasped my hand in a cow-milking grip. Possible loss of her bird crushed down on her, color drained from her face, and anxious hyperventilating heaves wracked her body. Her fingers seized a facial tissue and shredded strips instinctively into tight spitballs. Finally her voice focused. "Tell the inspector we have a friend in Brooking, Oregon, who wants a quail," she whispered hoarsely, "then we'll go back a few miles. I'll tuck Pedra in my dress and sneak through another inspector." Her tense mood was in full bloom.

But I agreed to the deception. A herculean bond, known only to mothers and daughters had developed between Betsi and the quail. We had traveled together nearly four thousand miles and fully intended to go home as a family.

67

The inspector twisted out of her booth, nibbling small brown scabs on her lip and I realized what an unattractive, self-important bureaucrat we had drawn. "Why," I moaned inwardly, "why had we entered her lane? Why hadn't we hidden Pedra?"

Her telephone investigation complete, the inspector swaggered from her booth and faced us. "No problem with your Gambel's quail," she told us with a friendly wave. What a decent official she had become with those words and I raised my eyes to Him for steering us into her stall. Her sunburned lips cracked as she smiled again and she glanced hesitantly at the heavy traffic gathering behind us. "Could I see your quail? Please could I see him? I love birds."

"Of course," Betsi said, reaching across the refrigerator and opening the apple box. "But he's a she and her name's Pedra." Pedra, who had reached a state of some exasperation during her incarceration, hopped immediately to the refrigerator and chattered as though she had drunk a couple of sherries.

Our friend—for by now I accepted her as a cherished ally—tiptoed forward and gasped. "She's beautiful! Hello, Pedra," she squealed through the sliding door.

I realized we were in the presence of an exceptional person. A family woman, I decided, with three small children at home. I generously added a fourth child, a daughter, blonde, sweet and dedicated as her mother. Her husband, I intuitively reasoned, had died tragically, perhaps in a smashing freeway pile-up while racing toward the birthing of their last child. I realized, as she leaned into the camper, what an infectious personality she owned. Marvelling that she could smile under her burden of widowhood, motherhood and official responsibility, I thought of recommending her as Mother-of-the-Year. Momentarily she seemed to have forgotten her personal tragedy and glanced at the other inspectors. "Hey, Fred, want to see something special?" she shouted.

Grapevine telegraphy flashed through the multiple stations and traffic stacked up in all lanes. Every inspector hurried to us and admired the young quail. Pedra did not disappoint them. Her quick chirps and staccato ramblings required answers and the inspectors replied with various cheeps and strange quail imitations.

One beanpole inspector loped toward us, peering through a slashing red scar that raced down his right eyebrow and nose and veered off his chin in a manner suggesting further damage under his shirt. He burst into a series of highly vocal bleeps and whistles the instant he spied Pedra. His bony arms flapped in the morning sun suggesting a stabbed chicken. Then the man pirouetted in wild silly circles, his head thrown back in ecstatic abandon all the while wailing his strange interpretation of a mating quail.

About fifty or so curious persons crowded around to watch the excitement. Most thought the crowd was due to either a drug bust or a movie celebrity. Half a dozen mongrel dogs joined the crowd sniffing and nipping legs but a peroxide blonde and her friend caused most of the trouble.

She cuddled a snow-white beribboned cat in her arms and softly comforted it while squeezing through the crowd. The increasing mob—now a hundred or so—pressed around the camper, trying to determine the cause of excitement. Wild rumors passed with satellite speed around us. "Cobras! A truckload of king cobras," was shouted back to the fringes. At that disclosure a number of older members faded back, but all the children and dogs pressed ever closer.

Under the circumstances even we double-checked the camper for suspicious wiggles, but none appeared. The chubby blonde, hemmed in by a sturdy gaggle of teen-agers raised her overfed cat and purred, "Look, Penelope, cobras!"

Penelope did not appear to be interested in cobras, but several dogs suddenly established an interest in Penelope. Like a stream of furry quicksilver they surrounded the vulnerable woman and leaped at her arms. Two of the larger beasts braced themselves against her shoulders and clawed at her dress. In reality they sought the snow-white feline in her hands, but in pursuit of that goal the dress suffered horrible casualties. Penelope squinted down on the attacking dogs with insolent green eyes, her back bent into an intimidating arch and she spat slobbery curses at her tormentors. Several smaller dogs, outclassed at the starting gate and unable to see the action, leaped and cavorted within the crowd and added to confusion by barking in higher octaves.

The woman could not defend herself since lowering Penelope invited disaster, so she continued providing a vertical beachhead for the attack on her pet. Her tattered dress draped limply and she intermittently coaxed the fragments together with a single hand. Her hat staggered crazily

69

over her eyes, but despite her temporary blindness she continued holding the hissing cat in one hand above her crying, "Penelope, Penelope, oh, Penelope!"

In view of the stiff competition, Pedra stopped chatting and simply stared at the spectacle. Horns thundered protest behind us and inspectors returned to their stalls. Our friendly official, bubbling with joy, leaned into the cab. "You'd better go," she whispered." I think everything will straighten out when you leave." Then she dropped her voice and confided, "I can't wait to tell Jerry about this. We've only been married a month and he simply loves wild things, especially me." She blushed at the unexpected confidence and bustled back, straightened her cuffs, and adopted an official face.

Trumpeting horns shoved us from the station and Pedra fluttered to the rear camper window for a rare curtain call. She usually did not believe in encores. We imagined her interest lay in Penelope, balanced high above in her owner's hand and still spitting at the yapping dogs. We too would have enjoyed a ringside seat for the final act but the pressure of traffic discouraged dalliance.

The VW bounded away as though embarrassed. Betsi's bottled-up laughter burst like warm champagne. A few miles later I discovered myself softly humming "Blue Bottle Fly" whose words I had never fathomed. Betsi mistakenly thought I hummed "Columbia the Gem of the Ocean" and her fallacy tossed us into another frenzy of laughter. The natural error inspired us to join in a duet of "Tom Dooley" celebrating the cause, and the highway echoed with our off-key version of the classic. Pedra rested her head on Betsi's lap, cocking an eye now and then at the landscape, completely innocent of having caused a near riot.

Plentiful quail food flooded the Redwoods and Pedra accepted it gratefully. Like a chain gang prisoner, she hobbled about camp, painfully tugging her pinecone anchor. Curious wandering ladybugs, resembling miniature psychedelic VW superbeetles, provided tasty meals. She pecked and sometimes caught pale yellow cabbage butterflies on the damp earth. Consuming the body first she then sucked in the tissue paper wings like a vacuum-cleaner. The wings were not consumed piecemeal, but in their entirety, the complete wafer disappearing methodically through the funnel in her throat. It seemed impossible! The gastronomic phenomenon so fascinated us we searched frantically for small butterflies, but they were not common in the dark forest.

After rains, thousands of slippery earthworms poked upward from snug subterranean condominiums. They offered easy pickings for Pedra, but she shunned that form of protein, preferring smaller centipedes and spiders. Under such ideal conditions she thrived.

Her physical appearance changed remarkably in two months with us. Bare traces of fluffy feathers remained. Especially sharp toes suggested she would be adept at perching but she was not. She, after all, was a flatlander. Preferring to rest on broad surfaces she teetered awkwardly on a wrist or stick, then quickly flew away. Promises of elegance sprouted from her head with the appearance of six new spidery, plume feathers. One morning the sun streaked through the redwoods, casting a halo on her face. Her top-knot tilted forward in classic quail fashion and she struck a pose that sent us racing for cameras. Now we knew. We had raised a beauty queen.

Snow-blocked Tioga Pass in Yosemite's National Park, our next destination, detoured us toward Death Valley, where winter storms blew fiercely across the bleak terrain. For the first time weather directly altered our plans.

I sat on a sycamore log sharpening my boning knife when thoughts of Sun City struck. I had been so completely absorbed with the marvel of travel that every thought of home vanished. Every road bend, every glistening dew crystal and each hidden waterfall invited investigation. My beloved herb garden, our Sun City friends and the intricate hummingbirds we fashioned from sterling silver and native stones lay buried beneath daily fantasies. Now they dramatically surfaced. I wanted to go home.

It had happened before. On a splendid morning in Guantajuato, Mexico, Betsi and I had breakfasted on green chili omelets when the same urge struck. Fifteen minutes later, after seven months in Mexico, we drove, not even pausing in Chihuahua to visit Pancho Villa's widow, to Juarez. Next morning we unlocked our door in Sun City.

Another time we aborted a carefully planned odyssey. After a year's search for a Caribbean tropical paradise, we awakened on Good Friday, 1979, to a spectacular sunrise. The sunrise proved to be St. Vincent's La Soufriere volcano erupting three and a half miles from our kitchen window. The explosion destroyed the home, all furnishings and a ripening crop of Big Boy tomatoes and wing beans. Never glancing back at the tannias, callaloo and water-nuts awaiting harvest, we hobbled over the mountains to the black-whale port at Barroullie, fifteen miles distant and scheduled the first flight home. Now homesickness overpowered me again.

"Let's go," I said to Betsi, carefully placing the knife in its leather sheath. She did not question why or where we were going. She knew.

Our avoidance of interstate highways was monumental. We believed in them for others, but mostly utilized sideroads for ourselves. Now we desired speed rather than scenery and discovered another unexpected facet of Pedra's personality.

She possessed an irrational fear of shadows! Riding in a shallow cardboard box secure on Betsi's lap, she enjoyed the rolling hills and small towns hidden from heavy interstate traffic. Suddenly a series of overpasses loomed ahead. We streaked under the concrete abutments and Pedra shrieked in terror.

At first we thought she might have been stung by a bee as she crouched in the gravel box awaiting doomsday. Wild, impatient wails flowed from her throat. Seconds later the next crossover appeared and again she shrank from death. Crying small helpless peeps of her childhood she cringed within the box. When the third overpass came in sight she dropped to the floor, defeated. Betsi picked Pedra up and cuddled her, whispering small comforting coos in her ear. Irrevocable, disastrous mental damage had occurred. Until we left the interstate and its terrifying overpasses, imaginary ghosts and gremlins sent gushes of panic into Pedra's craw.

In our long experience of pet ownerships many bizarre behavioral patterns puzzled us, but none was more startling than the unexpected miracle inside our camper while driving homeward. We looked back later and tried to remake the riddle into a logical pattern, but always failed. Nothing made sense. Was it sex, instinct or simply a whim resulting from a curious bend in the road? Eventually we stopped trying to explain the strange happening on Highway 93 that pleasant autumn afternoon.

The miracle exploded two hundred miles north of Sun City. We still talk about it. Pedra quietly scratched in the gravel box on Betsi's lap. Then suddenly, with no provocation, leaped to the steering wheel and hopped on my left shoulder. So sudden, so uncharacteristic was her movement both of us remarked about her unpredictable flutter. Never had she voluntarily moved to me when I drove. Now she perched dramatically close and warbled in my ear, or at least as close as a quail comes to warbling.

"Take her away!" I said rather irritably. "She bothers my driving."

Betsi reached behind my ear and returned Pedra to her lap, but the quail leaped instantly again to my right shoulder, marched around my neck and stared out the driver's window. She fixed firm sharp toes into my coarse tan sweater and remained anchored against my neck. She chattered in my ear while Betsi, slightly disturbed with her daughter's unexpected behavior, again leaned across and pulled Pedra into the lap box and held fresh sunflower seeds under her beak. Pedra ignored the bribe and fluttered back to my wrist. There she remained!

Never again would Betsi, who had snatched the chick from beneath a supermarket vegetable bin, claim even a small piece of Pedra's affection. The 5,000 mile trip of love, the intimate meals they shared, the daily clean bedding and fresh sand made no difference. She was mine!

A thunderbolt of love coursed through her young body and aimed her heart at me. I did not understand, but Betsi simplified the mystery. "It's that time of life. She needs a mate and you're the only male around."

I never had tried to coax her to me. In the beginning I had strenuously objected to her presence and had only recently realized Pedra to be a doubtful asset. Nor did I relish thoughts of a randy quail perched on my wrist warbling passionate love sonnets.

Now, despite a mountain of Betsi's love Pedra imprinted on me in a millisecond and that was that. Like a tiny sparkling pixie she fluttered about my shoulders watching over me like my guardian angel.

The full impact of the miracle did not sink in instantly. As we drove Betsi rattled pieces of chopped sunflower seeds toward Pedra, but she continued to ignored them. Betsi offered fresh water, but Pedra did not drink. Then we theorized my nubby tan sweater might be the attraction so at the first rest stop I removed it and placed the sweater between us. Pedra nestled comfortably into its folds and directed her alert dark eyes at me as though I might dissolve. We retested our theory again when Betsi slipped on my nubby sweater. Pedra scorned it and returned to my shoulder, sliding hazardously on the polyester shirt. Although her uncomfortable perch might have discouraged others, she did not return to the sweater. Thus we came to acknowledge she belonged to me. It was like unexpectedly receiving a lovely gift for which I had no earthly use. I was chosen!

An equally remarkable personality change surfaced. Pedra seldom spoke to Betsi again! Both girls had communicated from the beginning in sort of a quail-human language. We easily interpreted Pedra's coos and cheeps, and later, her raucous derisive invectives. Betsi could communicate with all birds and animals and with Pedra inside the camper they normally were a unique pair of magpies continually chattering—understanding each other.

The classic triangle devastated Betsi. No matter how hard she tried, Pedra did not talk, yet if I uttered the smallest sound, Pedra answered immediately. She seemed totally deaf to Betsi's speech, oblivious to her presence.

Her imprinting was in direct contradiction to normal birds. According to experts, imprinting usually happened at birth or shortly thereafter. Pedra waited two-and-one-half months. But Pedra was a different bird and her action not only disturbed Betsi, it broke her heart.

Pedra seemed more cheerful as we approached the desert. She leaped at times to the dashboard and peered into the low cactus-covered hills.

"She knows she's going home," Betsi explained.

Her answer startled me. "Impossible! She can't remember home. She was only a day old when she left."

But Betsi shook her head and I couldn't argue. It might be true. Pedra, certainly more alert after a long day's travel, flooded me with a torrential flow of conversation.

Our long journey neared completion. Saguaro cacti, like advancing infantrymen, guarded the desert while the aroma of mesquite and creosote filtered into the van. Jumping cholla squatted along roadside perimeters and finally our low white sister city, Sun City West, appeared. Our own comfortable bed only four miles away.

Crimson sunset flares shot through darkening clouds and, hypnotized by fatigue and a sense of relief, my foot pressed heavily on the accelerator. The number of familiar landmarks increased. We nodded at the Safeway store and lifted a hand in salute to saguaro-lined Bell Road. Then pausing at the Boswell stop light, seemingly forever red, we turned left and three blocks later touched the automatic door opener. The garage door swung upward and the dusty camper coasted inside, sputtering two small satisfied coughs.

Pedra, perched on my shoulder, peered at the unfamiliar interior, excited, curious and wondering. "Look, Pedra," Betsi whispered, waging battle with sentimentality, "this is Sun City. This is home. You're free now!" ➤

Chapter Ten

A quick patter of quail footsteps skittered behind me through the kitchen toward the carpeted patio. At the junction between rooms Pedra abruptly stopped. She critically inspected the thick patio carpet and—never having seen such luxury in a campground—a crippling reticence overcame her. It seemed an invisible enemy mine field lay ahead and she refused to face the danger. Her toes grasped the metal threshold and finally one leg advanced beyond the kitchen. Her large crooked toe touched the carpet much as a swimmer tests cold water. But she did not advance.

"Come on Pedra, it's only a rug," Betsi encouraged, for we were travel weary, anxious to inspect our home, soak in a hot tub and go to bed. But Pedra did not buy. She did not recognize the alien surface. Her head raised, she cocked a suspicious eye in our direction and glued both feet on firm kitchen tile. She apparently felt alone among invisible enemies.

Gingerly her foot probed toward the carpet. She glanced upward at us for reassurance then decided not to explore any farther. Glancing into the overgrown dark garden, only three feet away, she clearly would have felt more at home among the foliage and decorative pea gravel than on the rug. Any action seemed more desirable than a forced march on carpet pile.

Great decisions apparently raced through her mind. She balanced on one foot, her head cocked, her heart in conflict with the new environment. Mesmerized, she perched motionless facing the rug in the same manner as Columbus must have faced during his first voyage to India. Vague horizons and many unknown landmarks faced her.

Suddenly she hopped onto the rug and pecked three or four times as though searching for bugs. She quickly completed the reconnaissance, pointed her head upward as if examining a band of hawks, then weaved her neck from side to side like a cobra watching a flute. We seldom had seen Pedra so timid or indecisive. Finally, her trance snapped and she hopped back onto the kitchen tile. There she stood, perplexed, scratching vigorously on the floor—an exercise in which she was champion—and settled down comfortably on the threshold, eyeballing the unknown dangers of deep carpet pile. Her initial reaction to the rug was one of numerous idiosyncrasies she never explained.

We left her contemplating the booby-trapped patio and checked the house. Everything seemed in order. On returning, Pedra had not moved a feather, but stood at full alert, sounding warning signals to herself.

Betsi broke the spell. With a celery leaf dangling in front of her beak, Pedra's stomach answered the call. She touched a single toe on the rug, then set her foot down. Carefully, as if stepping on spooky shadows, she advanced one step and promptly snagged a toenail. All zest for exploration vanished and, glancing up, she clucked as though telling us to take her back to the boondocks. Finally wiggling her leg, she extricated it from the quicksand carpet and immediately tucked it under breast feathers. There she balanced on a single foot, her eyes leaping from the celery to the carpet and finally to us, the second foot firmly trapped in woolen pile. A low desperate wail flowed from her throat.

We laughed and her civility completely evaporated. She shouted quick mournful clucks in desperation and a paroxysm of sneezing shook her entire body as she sank to the carpet, eyes closed, whipped. Betsi gently cuddled the bewildered quail and deposited her on the kitchen table, holding the celery leaf close to her beak. We never fathomed her strange indecision.

"It appears we'll have to get rid of the patio carpet," Betsi said without smiling. "Pedra doesn't like it." Pedra opened a grateful eye and pecked voraciously at the leaf. That was her way. In about fifteen minutes she relaxed, perfectly at home. Before the evening ended she crossed the carpeted patio many times without a sideward glance. Why?

During the next few days Pedra set about organizing us. First, she adopted the refrigerator top as home. She stood there for hours, sometimes on one leg, observing our activities. Rejecting the apple box and feather duster on arrival,

she scratched, pecked and oiled feathers atop the porcelainized refrigerator as though it was her castle.

Our home was never the same with Pedra around and we reexamined our motives for allowing her there. Emphatically we had promised that she should be free when we returned. We kept that commitment. Since cold weather had not arrived, our patio remained wide open to unrestricted travel during daylight. Yet Pedra mainly divided her hours between the garden and the refrigerator. She revelled in freedom, but always kept an eye on us. If we left her sight she instantly returned indoors. No matter her love for outdoor hunting, she returned to us like a homing pigeon at dusk. When the sun dropped below the garden wall Pedra walked through the patio doors and, in a series of leaps and erratic flights, scratched to the top of the refrigerator.

Her arrival at the reefer top was no easy task. She attained it only by leaping to a ladder-back chair, then turning and scrambling to the kitchen counter. There she paused, checking bearings, always examining the refrigerator three feet away. The increased altitude thwarted her more than once and she fell, tumbling, to the floor. A moment later, after catching her breath, she tried again. If she didn't succeed the third time, Betsi set her, kitten gentle, on her bed. Pedra never offered so much as a thank-you, although if I assisted she warbled arias of gratitude.

Once on top, she scratched the bare surface as though digging a foxhole, looking in all directions. Then she hunkered down. Believing herself secure she dozed lightly, but kept an eye on Betsi who usually brought her a pre-dinner snack of sunflower seeds or a cut-up scallion. Again, with no thanks.

Since she enjoyed the refrigerator, Betsi decided to improve Pedra's diggings. She placed a small, towel-lined fruitbox on the refrigerator and carried Pedra to her new home. Pedra refused it. Betsi moved the bed back a few inches to a more secluded spot, but Pedra's rejection was firm and instantaneous. In desperation, and surmising Pedra wanted to keep us constantly in view, Betsi moved the bed to the very edge and waited for Pedra to clap her wings in joy. Instead she shrieked her indignation and strode around the refrigerator top muttering vague quail messages. Then she completely abandoned the lined fruitbox and flew to the patio. A rebellious fire burned in her soul and she showed little signs of extinguishing it.

After about ten excited laps around the patio, she rejoined us in the kitchen still muttering protests. Betsi stared in amazement when the independent little bird fluttered directly to the book-lined wall near the kitchen telephone. She perched precariously on the one-inch ledge in front of the books. Somehow she leveraged to the top of a book and squeezed inside like a spelunker, staring adventurously down at Betsi from her claustrophobic niche. One toe fiercely clasped *How to Cook and Eat in Chinese*, the other foot grasped *The Great Potato Book*. Her incredibly uncomfortable position bothered her not one whit. She shoved further into the tiny area, yawned and closed her eyes.

Betsi waved the white flag at the sight of Pedra clinging like a human fly to the bookshelf. She removed the bed from the refrigerator and apologized to Pedra. Then she lifted several books from the shelf (carefully, so Pedra was not disturbed, though she clucked warning signals anyway) and placed the rejected bed in the shelf. Then, as though she was in good with the Lord, Pedra strode pleasantly to bed, nodding a grateful acceptance to me.

From her high perch, inspection for ghosts and shadows was a snap; she apparently found comfort among the cook books. Then looking down, she saw us, closed her eyes and dreamed. An expression of delight crossed Betsi's face as she gazed admiringly at the little quail. "It was the penthouse or nothing. That girl's got class. Literary, too."

Her sleeping habits amazed us. Shortly after eight o'clock, she yawned and looked for a bedtime snack. Filling her craw from the gravel-filled shoebox on the counter, she relaxed. Small, happy coos continued throughout the snack and encouraged us to keep the box filled with seeds, sand and gravel. A gooseneck lamp over the box warmed her so she grew increasingly relaxed and her beak opened widely in frequent jaw-breaking yawns.

When her craw filled she sank into the gravel and stretched contentedly. Her legs extended far behind, lying on one side lazily pecking at a stray morsel. Glazed eyes slowly closed several times like a sleepy child—although they quickly popped open at any strange noise—and finally she relaxed as completely as any cat. After a minute or two, as though saying goodnight she would slowly rise, stretch full length, scan the bookshelf area several times, and fly directly to bed. She would turn counter-clockwise three times—no more, no less—and snuggle, facing us, into the cotton batting. Her eyes drifted shut several times, she clucked quietly, and slept until dawn. Only later did Pedra require a curtain in front of her sleeping quarters.

We never understood why she could fly to the top bookshelf at first try, yet fail to reach the refrigerator a foot lower. Did the refrigerator present invisible barriers not seen by us? In the early days the refrigerator certainly threw roadblocks at her and induced more failures than successes. No matter, she continued keeping the refrigerator a favorite spot except at bedtime. Why? Pedra never told us everything.

If friends visited and remained beyond eight o'clock, her procedure remained constant, flying to bed on schedule. If we talked and laughed loudly, an initial quieting cluck calmed us, but if noise continued she demonstrated firm authority. The kitchen television directly below her bed offered low volume entertainment, but occasional eardrum shattering episodes occurred after she retired. It shocked her sleep pattern. Naval battles, car crashes and shoot-outs popped her saucy black eyes open and she advised us to silence the damned noise.

In deference to Pedra's beauty sleep we sometimes moved to the living room for Monday night football and Saturday night Mexican boxing. She slept better under that arrangement. We also entertained friends who enjoyed life and manifested that enjoyment with rousing belly laughs. Sometimes Pedra was not amused. Late one evening guests grew increasingly loud and she suddenly fluttered from bed— we hadn't heard her caustic warning cheeps—flew into the livingroom and pranced in front of us. She scolded briefly and stomped out of the room, muttering to herself. We wondered who headed the household as Pedra continued stamping her personality on our lives.

Early one morning Betsi placed a large antique framed mirror on the floor under the table and waited for Pedra. The quail was stalking imaginary beetles on the carpet, but eventually crossed near her reflection. At first she barely glanced at it then, on second thought, stopped. Her eyes, never designed for darkness, experienced a sense of surprise and she stepped toward the mirror. The reflection fascinated her and she inched closer to see an immature female Gambel's quail staring at her in the shadows. She did not recognize the beauty facing her, who stared back. She did not realize her image had been described as one of the most beautiful ground birds in all North America. A twig snapped outside and she barely noticed, for she sensed the protection of the table above. Although insignificant sounds set her defenses aquiver, the inside room and table calmed her native suspicion and she continued carefully observing her reflection. She saw a family oriented bird who loved her mate above all others, a bird who shared familial duties with her partner equally. If death snapped the union—God forbid—she was prepared to accept full responsibility for nesting, food procurement and family training without question. Although her childhood had been abnormal she sensed the need for play periods, her sense of fun and frolic would never disappear and, even though most humans might not know, she possessed a sense of humor rivaling any bird in the land.

The quail in front of her weighed about six or seven ounces with enough flesh to attract game hunters. In Arizona two and a half million of her relatives had been harvested in a single year. Sturdy running legs supported her and she inherently walked or ran, rather than flew when startled. She did not understand why. It seemed the safest manner to avoid danger. Broad, powerful toes assisted her during brief flights and with them she pulled herself to tree branches and scratched for food and bathing areas. Actually, her toenails remained blunt with constant use.

She owned a black beak and brown eyes, although most people would call them black. Her eyes sparkled with deep curiosity regarding most things and her eyelids opened from bottom to top. Her blueish-gray body blended into mesquite and creosote bushes when she nested and her characteristic top-knot swung impudently forward in the manner of all quail. Pedra did not understand adjectives. "Dazzling", "glowing", "magnificent" or "svelte" were words unknown to her, yet she epitomized all. She was not so beautifully marked as her future mate, but she did not care. Nor did she ever care. In no sense was she self-important. Pedra inspected her image no closer than a quail's length then walked away and never again approached the mirror.

Potty training was another matter. In the farthest cranny of our conscience we had never considered quail house training. Now that problem leaped to top priority. We approached it quickly because it dropped, not unexpectedly, in our laps—and all over the house.

Actually we realized birds enjoyed a rapid metabolism. Since they consume massive quantities of food for their weight, they eliminate quickly, but quail, like most birds, possess clean and fastidious habits. Stepping backwards to the edge of the nest during elimination, they drop their deposits outside. The solution, in nature, is neat and practical. But once out of the nest, the world is their rest room.

We visualized sweeping droppings once or twice daily with an index card and depositing them into small birdie-bags. But our visions were quickly shattered. Sometimes they spattered. Secondly, her bombing area ranged far afield and included most unlikely targets. Picture frames, lamp shade interiors and even the bathroom sink bore evidence of her metabolism. My mind wandered back to a clean living room, an unspotted carpet and picture frames without capsuled surprises. Something had to be done.

I hurried to the library and faced a volunteer behind the information desk. She appeared exceptionally thin with gray hair tugged severely over her scalp and stapled in place with short brown and green combs. Sad, blue eyes and a long narrow face presaged anxious years of lonely companionship with books. I approached with optimism for she seemed the ideal person to assist me.

"I've got a Gambel's quail in the house," I began by way of introduction.

Patient, long years in quiet rooms tempered her display of interest but she slowly raised her eyes and fingered a card index file which would supply information should her memory fail.

"She—my quail—needs potty training. It's really quite messy." I shrugged my shoulders in an air of defeat and stared with my if-you-can't-help-me-nobody-can look. My helpless male act always drew raves and claimed a 98 percent success rate.

Hovering fingers halted over the index file and her pale eyes met mine. She swallowed two or three times searching for saliva. Finally, she rasped as though speaking through a tunnel. "Potty train a quail?" Her voice did not seem real.

Mountains of remorse overwhelmed me for having dumped another problem in her lap. She seemed the type of person born into multiple disasters, so I attempted to soften the puzzle. "Would you have books on the subject—or advice?"

"No," she said with some reluctance. "We have books on most subjects, but none on that." She spoke the word as if it was obscene. "Maybe you should try a psychiatrist." Her fingers drummed a tattoo on the polished desk and she seemed lost in thought.

"You mean a pet psychiatrist?" I asked, instantly regretting the question.

"No, a real psychiatrist." Her eyes focused someplace between the wall clock behind me and infinity. Then, abandoning my cause, she smiled weakly at the lady behind me and I stumbled away.

Betsi met me at the door. "We've got to put diapers on that bird," I shouted.

"Solutions will come," Betsi said kissing me on the cheek and chuckling to herself. "Let's think like a quail."

While we were thinking like quail Pedra continued eliminating like a quail and we studied her traffic pattern. She ate, digested and eliminated mostly around food dishes, so the next morning we placed *The Arizona Republic* under her dish and waited.

She was no *Republic* fan and joined us outside its perimeter at the kitchen counter for her dirty work. We covered the counter with *The Wall Street Journal*, but her interest in finance had never been intense and we followed, without difficulty, her excretory trail to the patio. Betsi draped the entire patio with old editions of the *News Sun* and she immediately scratched through the newsprint and delivered superb capsulated droppings into the soft carpet.

Our expectations, soaring on a mountain of false optimism, plummeted to the valley of reality, and we began to think like humans again. "That quail's got to go," I ordered.

"That's the problem," Betsi replied smiling. "She goes all the time."

Betsi devised sixteen methods of housebreaking Pedra at the deepest level of her conscience. All failed. One morning at breakfast she pressed her temples and meditated in front of an empty oatmeal dish. "Pedra likes soft cloth," She reasoned. "I know what to do." She nodded to herself and headed for the grab bag in the garage.

We extricated bags of colored cloth scraps, patched the entire patio floor, and for several days walked on a rainbow of rags. Horrid unsanitary and unsightly results appeared. Pedra managed to dodge most of the patches and flew to the couch or lamp for multiple, daily deposits. Also, retrieval of the colorful mess offered problems when neighbors dropped by. We intended maintaining as sane a profile as possible within the condominium and Pedra's presence didn't help.

Impromptu visitors, not neighbors, were murder. A Goodwill collector caught us unaware one bright Monday morning to pick up an unwanted pasta maker. He stared at the colored clutter on the floor and left without comment, or the pasta maker. Another day still stamped in memory, a genial florist entered the garden delivering a dozen long-stemmed roses. Stopping at the glassed patio doors, he watched Betsi toss multicolored remnants on the carpet. Nearly completing her task she noticed the man gazing awe-stricken through the glass. She continued placing a few more swatches and waved him inside. Normally cheerful, he seemed to have experienced a slight stroke for color drained from his cheeks and his hand trembled slightly while offering the receipt book. His eyes searched the floor for a reasonable solution. The sight of a mature woman flinging colored scraps randomly about the house seemed to depress him and retard conversation.

Betsi did not notice the man's dilemma for the scraps had become commonplace to her. She still carried a few pieces in her hand and glanced to see if any areas remained unguarded. Satisfied, she turned her attention to the man and said, "We're trying something."

The florist nodded agreement and tiptoed through the rags, kicking as he advanced, and set the roses down. Conversation seemed difficult for him but he smiled weakly and asked as though inquiring about terminal cancer. "You color-blind lady?" Then he escaped rapidly through the sliding doors carrying three pieces of mauve polyester on his boots. He sent his apprentice son on the next delivery to our home.

Betsi's soft-cloth theory proved excellent with only a single flaw. It didn't work. Pedra dodged the rags easily. In a spirit of realism Betsi prepared to admit failure when, one afternoon, above the whine of passing jets, a scream of joy filled the patio, "She hit it! She hit the red one three times!" she shouted with a ring of victory in her voice. Pedra certainly had.

We replaced several drab pieces with red patches and Pedra responded beyond our fondest dreams. We could hardly wait for her next capsule, dug out a red Christmas tablecloth and spread it in the center of the floor. Her fifty percent average enthralled Betsi until I pointed out Pedra had missed fifty percent, too.

We conferred over tea next morning and watched Pedra stalking the back of the couch. "She likes that spot. I'll concentrate there," Betsi said with some confidence. While I ridiculed the idea, Betsi draped the arms and back of the couch with the red Christmas table cloth. Pedra loved the texture, color and location. She spent a good deal of time aboard the couch and we reasoned the more time spent there the less she spent on the carpet, lamps and drapes. Our problems dramatically diminished. It was plain even to me that our color-blind bird favored the red tablecloth.

"Now if we can train her to spend half-time outside and the remainder on the couch our problem is solved," Betsi figured. And that's the way it happened. The long and high-backed couch allowed her to exercise and see throughout the garden. It easily became her favorite indoor area. She was happy and so were we. True, we cleaned periodic droppings, but that presented no problem. Her potty training had been hectic but brief. In two short weeks Pedra completely trained us, and throughout her life remained totally innocent of further toilet discipline.

Chapter Eleven

Our bittersweet tug-of-war over Pedra's fate continued. The campaign to release her raged within us and we faced the battle with a coward's heart. Her capture as a hyperactive chick—in an instant of impulse and opportunity—lay buried in the history of a lost summer. Betsi's thrill on scooping an infant quail to her bosom and smuggling it through the supermarket check stand was tempered by three solid months of companionship. She loved the renegade. All this despite Pedra's recent reluctance to return Betsi's affection. Our infant, now nearly full grown and in love with me, lived as a squatter in our house. We faced a painful reassessment of our original attitude.

True to our promise, we completely freed her. She did not leave, but we expected a flight over the wall any day for she grew more confident with successive sunrises. Prancing male quail raced around neighboring walls calling teen agers to their side and we thought Pedra listened. As much as we expected her early departure we secretly hoped she would stay. Well, at least a few more days.

One afternoon I entered the kitchen, my arms overflowing with groceries, and I sensed I was not alone. In a moment my eyes became accustomed to subdued light and I perceived Pedra perched on the drain rack solemnly watching me. She had been waiting. As I pulled groceries from bags, Pedra stepped across the sink and offered a bashful cheep as though not certain of her welcome. I answered and continued stacking provisions on the breadboard when Pedra hopped atop a bottle of pickled artichoke hearts. She did not continue visiting, but watched with inquiring black eyes and stepped timidly toward me as if to say something of great importance. Then quite suddenly, she impulsively fluttered to my shoulder and pressed against my neck, resting quietly on one leg. There she cuddled! So on that fine autumn day, when massive dry fig leaves fell in loud clusters on pea gravel outdoors and rustled across the yard I felt a comforting warmth enter our home and it was not associated with the automatic furnace.

Outrageous selfishness entered my heart. If the truth were known I would have traded my soul to keep the young bird. When she attached herself to me in the camper she staked a solid claim to my heart, my time and my life. The sentiment was mutual. If I left the room she cried desperate long wails. Her pattering feet followed me throughout the house and, although she remained quick as a cat, we exercised great care not to step on her, for she was constantly underfoot. She leaped to my lap and together we read magazines and newspapers, although at times she demonstrated exasperation with the length of certain articles. She did not care for books, for they contained few pictures, but hopped to the top of the novel and balanced as I read, registering mild complaints when I turned pages. Mostly she chattered soft conversations and her eyes always followed my every move.

Yet Pedra owned complete liberty except for an intangible thread of friendship. With our patio door open, absolute freedom faced her outside. We encouraged outdoor life and she selected special bathing, pecking and hunting areas in the garden. She enjoyed strolling through thyme plants, circling overgrown rosemary, and discovering fat green worms, remaining outdoors as long as she could see us. Let us disappear and Pedra scrambled inside with such speed that we often worried that a hawk or fox had discovered her home. Excitement and fear disappeared once she reached the patio and she relaxed completely, pecking at imaginary rug insects and double-checking that we had not dissolved. Then she returned to the garden. After two weeks we declared she had become too dependent on us and decided to act.

Next morning Pedra strolled, as usual, through the patio doors for her morning hunt. We closed the glass doors behind her. She cooed, scratched and happily searched among marigold blossoms, which are notorious for harboring delicious tiny, black beetles. Gradually we stepped from sight yet peeked into the marigold patch. Suddenly she did not see us and the world closed around her. She thundered frantically to the closed door, panic in her voice, and struck the glass at full speed. Quickly recovering, she whipped back and forth like a shuttlecock, pecking and searching for a secret entrance wailing five long minutes before we opened the door.

A quail's wail of despair is demanding. Phonetically the sound resembles "a-WAH-ha" and it is repeated so persistently we heard it in our sleep. Experts characterized the cry as "Chi-CA-go," but we labeled it "for-GOD'S-sake" and eventually capitulated after listening to her intense caterwauling.

She cried six minutes the second day outside closed glass doors and seven excruciating minutes—even developing a severe case of hiccups—before we admitted defeat the third day.

Pedra refused to leave the patio next day although the doors, as usual remained wide apart. Mostly she sat on the couch staring outside at a pair of visiting Rufus hummingbirds, a constant flow of hungry Inca doves and chattering finches. Several days later, sensing victory over us, she hesitantly resumed old hunting habits. After that Pedra roamed freely inside and out, coming in for water, fresh lettuce and sunflower seeds. We never closed doors on her again.

She loved dust bathes and could have written a book on its technique. Every day, and sometimes twice, she bathed outside, and her routine seldom varied. She chose a spot of soft loam under a canna or in the herb patch and tentatively scratched. If it did not meet her exacting specifications, she moved a few inches and tested another site. While pecking and scratching her dark eyes continually focused in our direction. If we moved from sight she quickly returned to the patio. As a result, one of us remained in her vision at bath time, but usually both joined her in the garden for it was a fine performance.

Dust baths apparently served a number of purposes, but cleanliness must have been the prime consideration, for she never showed signs of lice or other infestation. Bathing destroyed everything under her feathers! Simple rubbing might not have accomplished near-sterilization but for Pedra, bathing was no simple process. She pushed, shoved and grunted during her bath until no life dare exist. We watched in fascination.

The first time she bathed we held our breath in wonderment. She carefully selected a soft, slightly damp spot and pecked rapidly into the loam, thrusting her head sideways and tossing dirt a foot away. Then, with her oversized feet, scratched powerful scars into the earth. In a remarkably short period she fashioned a shallow dirt bowl under the flowers and began checking the tub for size and shape. She seemed most fastidious about the entire development and sometimes rejected a site after working on it several minutes. If the first site contented her, she persisted in pecking and scratching until a soup-bowl sized pit formed. Then the real show began.

She shouldered into soft loam and began a series of gyrations, her contortions equalled only by accomplished belly dancers. Wiggling and twisting in the hole, she tossed dirt high into the air then curiously coiled inside the bath and pecked vigorously under her breast, shooting small gravel, twigs and clods into surrounding vegetation. Her wings fluttered in powerful scooping motions and her large feet scratched deeper and deeper into the proposed bathing pool. Slowly she buried herself as dust settled around her. Preliminaries completed, Pedra readied for the actual bath.

Inside the soil bathtub her feet pressed tightly against the sides and she propelled dirt into her feathers. Turning from side to side Pedra forced abrasive particles against her skin, tossing dirt and sand into feathers with her beak and wings. Only a sandblaster could have been more effective. Dust flurries rose like a miniature atomic cloud around her.

With closed eyes she rolled backward, pressing against the tub bottom screwing about, shoving and cooing in rapturous delight, utterly abandoned to bathing pleasure. Betsi and I expected her, while on her back, to kick her legs in the air and whinny, but she was not a horse. She scoured her head non-stop against the tub's sides.. At times her head seemed twisted completely around while polishing her scalp against dirt walls and small rocks. The final act of bathing seemed instinctive. Her head, wings, beak and toes moved automatically, her mind drifting to heaven. She cherished every second. So did we.

Slowly, rhythmically, her action slowed. A gentle stillness settled around the canna clump, the autumn breeze glided to docile equilibrium and paused, cathedral quiet. Inside the garden as Pedra stretched her legs and feet full length, her head returned to its frontal position. Her wings relaxed and an exquisite state of well-being coursed through her body. Once more she resembled a young quail instead of a feathered pretzel.

Completely exhausted, Pedra lay motionless for a moment or two gathering strength. Slowly rising she shook feathers in a dusty explosion. Normally a sandy tablespoon or two of dirt burst from her feathers as she shook several times before crawling from her tub. Then, heading for the patio in slow determined steps, she advertised that she was finished. She heaved heavy sighs of contentment on arriving in the patio and dropped on the carpet, luxuriating like a cat in a sunbeam. An hour's powerful sleep was not unusual to restore her energy.

Sometimes she did not finish shaking outside and carried massive dirt accumulations to us in her feathers. With rapid, energetic body twists she detonated them over the carpet. It wasn't unusual for her to climb aboard my lap and toss a tablespoon of dirt in my face.. On these frequent occasions Betsi uncomplainingly brought the vacuum and cleaned the carpet and wiped the furniture. "It's the same as cleaning after kids," she said. "Or you."

Pedra required fifteen minutes to complete her toilet! We clocked her several times. Occasionally she took five or ten-minute spit baths but they only served as dry runs for the full Roman tub, sauna, rubdown and massage treatment.

Over a period of weeks Pedra developed numerous dust holes and the garden soon resembled a bomb-pitted battle-field. She especially enjoyed the herb patch directly in front of the kitchen window and nearly destroyed it with her phenomenal exercises. Only sturdy perennials, marjoram and rosemary resisted her toenails. Flowering plants, sprinkled among the herbs, ceased to survive for she ferreted out hopeful transplants of sweet alyssum and marigolds—which she especially savored from blossom-tip to root stem—and tossed remnants aside to die. Far from becoming exasperated, we welcomed her outdoor toilet, for during earlier days she sought inside bath facilities.

She selected, as her first indoor victim, a massive jade plant. Returning from shopping one fall afternoon we discovered the patio floor covered with dirt and jade plant fragments. The ancient shredded plant lay uprooted and dying on the carpet, its destruction herculean for the plant was generations old. Pedra completely demolished it in a single afternoon! She could not destroy the container—a sturdy clay pot, survivor of rampaging children since the turn of the century—but lazied within its confines in the sunny patio. She glanced up at us as though proud of her accomplishment and seemed completely happy and unaware of the horrid mess around her.

Her next victims were three prize amaryllis bulbs Betsi nurtured from season to season. They sprang from the potting soil one happy week, sending out succulent fresh green promising leaves and suffered death by mutilation before growing six inches high.

An exotic pot of lemongrass, loved for its subtle Oriental flavor, fell next. Pedra tossed the grass-like leaves throughout the room and littered the carpet with gravel, dust and dirt. We debated the location of her next strike, even casting apprehensive glances at the five-year-old fig tree in the garden. Betsi wondered if Pedra dared, under the magic of a full moon, tackle its four-inch trunk. But the fig tree survived.

Pedra also discovered prized African violets in Betsi's bathroom. She classified them with spinach, parsley and broccoli, nibbling leaves and petals until even an expert would have failed to identify their origin. When we complained to friends they offered no sympathy and classified us chronic imbeciles. In defense of our temporary idiocy we simply could not believe a six-ounce youngster could have destroyed our patio greenhouse.

In desperation Betsi dismantled the wire cage, veteran of the 5,000-mile camping trip, and cut and fitted metal guards around the base of all surviving plants. A badger would have been challenged to gain entrance through the wire. Pedra, too, was stymied and we felt victorious, but did not lower our defenses.

Sensing that the plants had not been her primary target, we figured an indoor surrogate tub might divert her attention. When she desired a bath she sensibly used the first container available. We blamed ourselves. Had we not left her alone, the destruction never would have happened for she would have gone outside to bathe. The entire fiasco belonged in our camp.

To correct our deficiency, Betsi filled the jade clay pot with soft loam and seated it in the patio inside a deep, oversized cardboard box with towering walls. Despite its forbidding abutments, Pedra flew instantly to the edge and drifted inside. The sound and fury of flying dirt filled the patio and she casually flung debris as far as the kitchen, 15 feet away. Next door neighbors heard quail arias of contentment through insulated walls. Generally, the giant clay pot posted a rousing success as an indoor bathhouse during inclement weather or times when she was left alone. With a temporary truce under her wing, she sought new frontiers.

One morning—without consulting us—Pedra scheduled a maiden flight atop the garden wall. Then, enjoying the view, she strolled along its borders and flew to the attached garage. At wing's length she inspected us with a superior attitude and despite our calls and offers of sunflower seeds, stalked back and forth without regard for our frustration. Fortunately her maiden voyage proved a quick round trip and she returned to the herb garden after inspecting the territory from her crow's nest.

Her flight telegraphed an early departure to quail relatives or—God forbid—a mate. Jealousy was not unknown in my heart and Pedra was, in my mind, still my child, not ready for a home of her own. Watching her on the garage, mixed feelings seized us for I prized her in a way that would have been unbelievable a month ago.

Once back on the ground she scratched vigorously at small pebbles by her feet calling low satisfied coo-coo-coos from beneath a sweet basil plant. Her continuous throating clucks, quiet and contented, implied explicit happiness for her world. Ours too.

A few nights later twilight came swiftly. Outside, Pedra scratched and searched for pre-dinner insects while we admired spectacular autumn storm clouds tumbling over the valley. A pair of hummingbirds dodged through the garden and Pedra, startled by the unexpected shadow, flew to the garage roof. Her action, not unusual, brought smiles to our faces for she had never forgotten overpass shadows. Without worry we continued examining a humpbacked thunderhead fingering its path toward us with terrifying speed.

Suddenly a chilling wind tore at our throats and the sky exploded in a blast of forked lightning, its tongue licking the desert floor. A murderous roll of thunder followed and a second lighting flash, more brilliant than the first, burst in a fiery explosion near the yard. I threw both hands defensively over my eyes. Thunder tumbled around us like an artillery barrage and instinctively we both called to Pedra. She did not answer. We ran to the alley and searched the tapering garage roof, but she was nowhere in sight. As we searched, a cold gusty squall spat oversized raindrops in our faces and we shouted frantically into the storm. Ear-splitting thunder rolled again, echoing repeatedly.

The delayed autumn cloudburst finally pinpointed its target and struck at us with spiteful fury. Within seconds solid sheets of water cascaded inside the court. Despite its intensity we searched for Pedra in the waterfalls and among low pfitzers, finally returning to the patio soaked and chilled. But Pedra was gone! Apprehension touched our hearts and we stared hopelessly at swirling debris filling the yard, threatening momentarily to tumble into the patio. Terrifying thunder jolted us and we jumped repeatedly, anticipating the next rumble. Under different circumstances we might have enjoyed the experience, but now each lightning strike plummeted our spirits.

Nature's temper calmed as quickly as it exploded, leaving us facing inky blackness and dripping leaves. Outside the wall, anxious freshets raced toward drainage canals and far away groaning thunder booms signaled the storm's departure. In dry clothes and raincoats we hurriedly searched for our little friend. Several times Pedra had raced over the roof and dropped into the common courtyard in front of the condominium. We splashed through puddles armed with flashlights and pried into bamboo, bottlebrush and lantana, calling frantically as darkness fell. Quail were known to roost in trees and we stabbed the blackness with light. Finally flashlights dimmed and so did our spirits. We reluctantly plodded home saturated with defeat.

Inside we sat quietly, huddled on the couch, blinking into darkness. Isolated puddles slowly disappeared and, in the quiet of night, heavy droplets splashed loudly from the fig tree. Although midnight had passed, dinner was out of the question. I spoke to Betsi, but she did not listen or answer. She sat sullenly alone, shaking her head in frustration.

Dead tired we waited for our second wind and evaluated Pedra's survival chances. She abhorred darkness, never walking through a darkened passage even to reach light.

Sometimes we did not return until after dark and Pedra refused to fly to bed if we had neglected to leave a nightlamp lit. Pedra could not, we thought, be far away unless she had bolted across the main street. In that event she was gone, gone, gone! In the darkness a sly smile wrinkled Betsi's tired face. "The butler did it," she said.

"What?" She's gone off the deep end, I thought, but Betsi smiled again and giggled with fatigue.

"The butler really did it. We've overlooked the obvious. Pedra's in the garden. We simply didn't find her during the storm."

Her presence there seemed too much to hope, but we flood-lit the yard and continued the search of Pedra's favorite hunting grounds. All favorite bath holes shimmered with fresh rain water, but we carefully probed them, methodically stalking through savory, basil, chives and thyme, all the while calling quietly to our bird. Betsi shook a plastic castanet of sunflower seeds to tempt her, but at one-thirty we admitted defeat. Pedra no longer roamed her garden.

Pains of loneliness spread through the quiet house and we noticed, for the first time, the absence of fresh stray feathers and friendly continuous chatter. Pedra ceased to exist except for her empty bed, the kitchen gravel box and her disreputable jade-pot dust bath. We fell into bed and lay together, not touching, listening to dripping rain from the Queen Anne palm outside the window. I embraced Betsi's thin wrist. Her pulse seemed erratic. "Are you all right?" I whispered.

"No," she said so quietly I barely heard. Suddenly she started crying and I forgot all previous antagonisms against the little quail and searched for words of comfort and love. A strangling impatience enveloped us and, without speaking, we both arose and dressed.

Betsi stirred hot spiced tea with slow sweeping motions and we nibbled on a pyramid of dry toast while analyzing Pedra's mind. She would not intentionally fly from us. Thunder had startled her and, terrified of water and darkness, she was lost or dead. But where? Grappling with the puzzle we firmly decided she could not be far away. If she lived we would find her; if she was dead funeral services would be arranged. But we would find her.

We probed rain-soaked trees and bushes slowly as we searched. Within minutes water dripped from us, too. An old aching chest pain surfaced, I breathed with difficulty and tried, unsuccessfully, to square my shoulders and face the hunt with confidence. Positive thinking had disappeared and Betsi slogged despondently behind. Systematically retracing a previous hunt in the courtyard, we sloshed toward the north condominium. Bush by bush and tree by tree we waited for Pedra's quiet voice. Our cautious calls remained unanswered. Only the southern condominiums remained. We had instinctively avoided those because a wild gray tomcat had staked claim there and stripped the area of finches, mocking birds and Inca doves. If Pedra drifted into his range we would be fortunate indeed to discover feathers to bury.

We stumbled in darkness. "It'll be a miracle if she survived the storm and the tomcat," Betsi mumbled. "I know she's gone." No comforting answer came.

My infantryman's eyes searched dripping bushes in Lace Court with little hope. While disconsolately probing among great patches of bougainvillea a faint chirp erupted. I did not believe my ears but called, "Ped...Pedie...Pedra? Is that you?" Again a faint reply. Bending into the saturated foliage I barely saw her small cold form anchored in mud at the roots of a flowering bottlebrush. Defenseless blinking eyes stared blankly at me. "Here's Pedra," I called.

"Is she all right?"

"Don't know. But she's here."

Betsi ran with passion through the dripping darkness and dove into sopping leaves. When she arose Pedra lay in her hands, eyes wide and dull with fear. She shrank into Betsi's fist with small, unfamiliar sounds and whimpered explanations. Snuggling deeper into Betsi's palm, she appeared half normal size—almost like a sparrow—and barely alive.

Dawn's first light broke fresh and pure through wet palm trees and the tender morning promised a magnificent late autumn day. Drunk with relief we carried Pedra home. Honest-to-God coffee brewed and bacon sizzled in a nearby condominium and we enthusiastically inhaled its perfume. Pedra was back!

"She's on the side of angels!" Betsi glowed and lovingly rubbed the dripping quail with a soft dishtowel. She played the hair dryer in lazy swirling figures around the young bird and offered warm water. Pedra's feathers slowly dried, her voice strengthened and within an hour trembling legs supported her six-ounce body. Then she stood, stretched and shook feathers at us.

"She's probably caught a cold," Betsi fretted. "We'll keep her in the house a week or so."

"No we won't," I argued. "If she were wild she'd have survived and she's almost grown. Pedra goes outside today. If she catches pneumonia, that's life."

Betsi's lip puckered briefly then firmed with determination. "She isn't wild and she isn't grown. We'll keep her inside!" Her emphatic statement charted the first time either of us admitted Pedra might not be wild. It also revealed she might be our permanent guest. ➤

Chapter Twelve

The next morning Betsi waited for me in the kitchen, a rare occasion indeed, for she enjoyed the last hour's sleep more than all others while I tumbled from bed at the crack of dawn, challenging each day. Despite sleepy eyes her face radiated the splendor of a rainbow and she threw her arms about me and kissed with strength that left me gasping. A heated plate of scrambled eggs and bacon waited on the table. She had not treated me that way in years. Her explanation clarified everything. "Pedra's home again. We've got our girl."

Surprisingly, except for our worry hangover and sleep deficit, we had little to show for last night's drama. Pedra displayed no signs of fatigue or stress. None. Her magical presence filtered again throughout the house with brief fluttering journeys to favorite corners and chirrupy conversations with herself and me. She gave Betsi not a second glance much less a grateful thank you.

She strolled around the garden snapping at passing ants as though nothing had happened. If able to talk she might have wondered what all our fuss was about. Instead, dustbaths in the jade clay pot occupied her attention, for the earth outside was much too wet. Toward evening she cocked her eye at finches disputing ownership of an overripe fig, all memory of thunder, lightning and raging waterfalls completely forgotten. Betsi uncorked her deceptive smile that stretched from ear to ear and said, "I knew Pedra wouldn't leave us. She wouldn't miss Thanksgiving."

Indeed she wouldn't! Barely five months old, Pedra claimed teenage status. Shiny blueish-gray and cream colored feathers adorned her body and half a dozen black feathery plumes projected spunkily from her head. She controlled her top knot in any direction, but generally it tapered forward in accepted quail fashion. Her oversized feet and legs continued growing and could have supported a young ostrich. We wondered if God had not mismatched those appendages with an emu, but no matter. Pedra was, in our opinion, strikingly beautiful.

Thanksgiving had always been a special holiday. When we migrated a thousand miles to Sun City, pleasant memories and gluttonous appetites travelled with us. Every year we sank happily into a deep culinary rut of roast turkey, sage dressing and candied sweet potatoes—for starters. Betsi rediscovered her mother's hundred-year-old mince pie recipe and we baked my mother's secret pumpkin pie (made with Golden Hubbard squash) classic. Savory side dishes and appetizers bulged the Thanksgiving table as well as our figures. We hid bathroom scales until February and buried ourselves in a ruinous diet.

Pedra loved every busy minute as though the excitement was orchestrated for her alone. Early in the week she frolicked in a tub of drying cornbread croutons marked for sage dressing, flinging the cubes about like exploding popcorn. I swept the soiled cubes into the garbage and quickly oven-dried another batch, this time hiding them from her. We wondered about the strange noise in the garage next day and discovered Pedra once again ecstatically bathing in the crouton tub "hidden" on top of the washing machine.

I raced to the garage and Pedra looked up. Croutons lay everywhere. It seemed she almost smiled and in frustration I shouted at her. She remained at attention about a second, for I seldom raised my voice, then scratched cornbread into my face with several powerful piston-like strokes. A glow of happy contentment framed her face and, apparently in deference to my consternation, she slowed scratching and, gently, tossed the last croutons at me. Then she leaped to the bowl's edge and stared happily into my face. Hers was a gesture of proud accomplishment I would long remember. Betsi hastily baked a third batch of cornbread and carried it to a cooperative neighbor for safekeeping.

Cranberry relish preparation proved especially memorable. Pedra cast wild anticipatory glances at the lemon-orange-cranberry treat, She fluttered to the bowl's rim and ate so greedily we prepared a special dish just for her. Then Betsi made additional relish so guests would not be deprived. Pedra's shimmering excitement quickly passed to Betsi whose face lit up with each successive prank.

We should have jailed her during lefse baking. Her abundant enthusiasm nearly destroyed all our efforts to complete an old and enjoyable family custom. We cooked several huge chilled bowls of Scandinavian, calorie-filled potato pancakes on a broad cast-iron skillet during a three-night bake-off. We always baked enough lefse for the entire holiday season. But those were pre-Pedra nights.

She took a fancy to lefse production at once and thrilled at the danger beneath the giant rolling pin pressing across the floured board. Each time she barely escaped severe damage as the roller crossed her path, then she nimbly hopped atop the roller at the last minute. But the real danger lay on the steaming bake-griddle, and that was her preferred location. Leaping to the center of the pancake as soon as it unfolded on the stove, she nibbled on hot crusty edges, and hopped from foot to foot, while it cooked. She particularly enjoyed the pleasure of rising briefly on a bubble as the pancake rose and browned, all the while expressing pleasure with rapid, enthusiastic chirps. On the rare occasions when she decided to rest, large, floured walking tracks and a cloud of white dust marked her exit. Lefse baking was, for Pedra, a night at the carnival!

I reprimanded her constantly, (she was a horrible nuisance) yet she had an impudent way of cocking her head with one eye looking through me and giving the impression of intense concentration for a second or two, then completing her impromptu mischief. After four evenings of lefse baking—an extra evening became necessary with her help—we banished her to the bedroom. Frantic last minute preparations faced us and we could not afford more of Pedra's assistance.

Thanksgiving morning Pedra raced to the garden, threaded through a gap of parsley, under pine-scented rosemary and squatted beneath a clump of French tarragon, watching wildlife in her yard. A skittering, noisy band of finches soon fluttered down, searching for grain supplied by Betsi as a special Thanksgiving treat. Pedra instantly flapped her wings and issued a raucous reprimand. Not choosing to challenge her authority the finches scattered over the wall. Then, having tested the pecking order, she searched for her bathtub. I hoped she would spend the entire morning there because much preparation was yet to be done and we did not need Pedra's eager help.

I assembled sage stuffing in a giant metal bowl normally reserved for Superbowl popcorn when a feathery alarm sounded behind me. Pedra sprang to the table. She surveyed the semi-dry croutons, chopped celery and onions then dropped in feet first like a paratrooper. Furiously scratching and pecking as though she had not eaten since Lent, she flew outward to the bowl's lip and chirped onion fumes in my face. Her near destruction of a proud dish triggered a reflex and I backhanded her to the floor. Neither of us previously had touched her in anger. Only my overwhelming size and Pedra's amazement stopped her from retaliating. Instead, she severely lectured to me while walking around my feet in rapid figures of eight.

I busied mixing chicken broth, baking powder, eggs and sage, wondering if I shouldn't banish her to the garden when the devil twisted her heart again. She flew behind my back in a miracle of aerial acrobatics and landed dead center into the mixing bowl. Instantly she scratched a quart of dressing on the floor and prepared to toss the remainder outside too, accepting it as an ideal bathing area.

I had been watching most carefully, but her complete innocence surprised me. Breast-deep in stuffing, her curious eyes challenged me, for she always stared directly at me as though expecting an argument. She hiccupped onions again in my face—this time with a dash of garlic—and, deciding the bowl did not provide satisfactory conditions, hopped over to the table. Betsi swept the floor and bathed Pedra's feet. I prayed enough dressing remained for dinner.

We wondered about her response to the large group of celebrants because she never had been exposed intimately to groups larger than four. We worried needlessly. Initially Pedra's exemplary deportment amazed us, for she paraded regally among guests chirping and preening. Few had ever chatted with a Gambel's quail on family terms, much less one with garlic breath. Pedra had refreshed her craw with a whole garlic clove moments before guests arrived and stank mightily.

She nimbly hopped from guest to guest, paying homage to all, but special attention to those with dangling earrings and flashing bracelets. She was so deceptively charming we succumbed to temptation and granted her dining room privileges while we ate. At the last moment common sense prevailed and, based on her pre-Thanksgiving pranks, we secured her in the glass-walled bedroom.

She reacted violently, racing back and forth between the drapes and glass door, hurling continuous blasphemies at us. "For-GOD'S-sake, for-GOD'S sake, for-GOD'S-sake," she wailed a thousand times. Her protest march achieved instant attention, her bushy plume sprang to attention and her throat vibrated passionate throbs. In about four minutes all sympathy flowed into Pedra's camp for appetites dampened under the influence of her heartbreaking cries. Pleading guests coaxed us to remove her from isolation. So with a prayer in our heart, we released her on good behavior. Again we need not have worried. Definitely chastened she slowly circled the table waiting for an invitation that never came. Although nonplussed at our snobbishness, she clucked happily while we ate, darting in for an occasional dropped crumb. She kept us company until dessert time, then disappeared.

Moments later Betsi entered the kitchen then motioned to me with a quiet finger. Pedra greeted us knee-deep in the shallow gravy pan, wading ecstatically among giblets, her eyes challenging reprimand. We thoroughly baptized her feet under the faucet and, squawking furiously, separated her from grease and gizzards without disturbing the others.

Blotted dry, she was banished to the rear bedroom—one without glass doors—to prevent further mischief until moments before guests left. Released, she flew to the patio and clucked goodbyes so charmingly that everyone gushed about what a well mannered quail we owned. They were wrong on two scores. She had not been well-mannered and we did not own her. Quite the contrary. She held title to us.

We also challenged Pedra's good behavior medal, purposely neglecting to tell guests she had made another unscheduled kitchen trip and investigated pumpkin pies. She left oversized tracks in both and huge dollops of whipped cream expertly covered her marks before we served dessert.

Pedra did not arise with me next morning. Her abrupt and muted greeting signaled a change in attitude, for she normally greeted me cheerfully. Perched high in her bed she observed me reading *The Arizona Republic* without comment. Silence did not come easily to her, but like all individuals she enjoyed a degree of privacy at times. I blamed her temporary hush on Thanksgiving gluttony, but was surprised when she refused morning cream of wheat.

When she finally joined us late that morning her sad glazed eyes suggested Alka Seltzer. By nightfall, with dismaying clarity, we realized Pedra was sick. Not once during the day had she challenged us and at bedtime her voice remained depressingly still. Placing the blame on whipped cream, a special delight and much too rich, we bedded her, telling each other that tomorrow she would be better.

Lifting her to bed she stood on one leg and sneezed several times. Her fluffed feathers gave the appearance of a small feather duster, nearly twice normal size. Her eyes closed slowly and she remained motionless without interest in us or fresh broccoli. Listlessness did not characterize her and we prayed she would recuperate by morning, for we had suffered identical post-Thanksgiving symptoms many times.

The next morning Pedra refused fluids and her ice-cold feet—normally warm—raised the warning flag. Yawning continuously her fluffy body quietly sank to the carpet and anchored itself in deep pile. Morning hunting and dust bathes were abandoned and our encouraging calls, when we passed through the patio, remained unanswered. She seemed uncomfortable, but without undue distress and, though concerned, we didn't worry. Since her initial baby dehydration Pedra had never known a day's illness. By early afternoon another series of small sneezes shocked her and she rose only by fits and starts. At sundown she could not walk. Betsi forced several drops of medicated water along her beak bringing neither resistance nor cooperation.

"She's got a cold. A bad one," I diagnosed.

"We've got penicillin. Let's give her some." Betsi usually included penicillin in her magic three-medicine kit. Aspirin, milk of magnesia and penicillin lay, ready for action, in a small container and any illness not responding to those three required intensive care. Fortunately we were never ill and the tablets decomposed, smelling of lemon essence and hangover bile. The small milk of magnesia bottle had long lost its identity, but Betsi shook it every year or so with the same speculative curiosity Madame Curie might have employed while inspecting early radiographic films.

"Penicillin has never cured a cold," I told her for the thousandth time. "Penicillin kills bacteria, not viruses."

"Well," she snorted, abandoning all thoughts of help from me or her magic kit, "I'm going to Phoenix and find medicine that will help. Our quail is sick!" She washed her face, combed her hair and straightened her dress in a near-single motion, then scurried away before I could answer. She had a disconcerting habit of implementing action before I could object. It was a custom I found confusing.

Pedra nestled quietly in my hand, her body heaving in exaggerated efforts to gain oxygen and she yawned continuously. Within an hour Betsi returned toting erythromycin capsules and vitamins especially compounded for respiratory ailments. That, apparently was Pedra's problem. Conversation with the pet store salesman and two passing bird lovers had diagnosed, quite willingly, Pedra's illness. I didn't disagree, for Pedra needed help. Immediate help.

Betsi emptied two capsules into a cup of warm water. "This is a five-day supply," she explained and pressed an erythromycin saturated cotton swab into Pedra's beak. Pedra instinctively closed her mouth and swallowed. Half-choked with liquid she sneezed three times, shook her head and slowly sank to her knees.

An overwhelming weakness paralyzed Pedra and she barely moved when Betsi gently lifted her to the high bookshelf. A pool of emptiness surrounded her, finally enveloping the entire house. Even the refrigerator, normally comforting in its defrosting cycle, remained stubbornly quiet. We lay in bed listening to nightbirds and praying for Pedra's recovery. In blackness I felt a purge of tears on Betsi's cheek as winter's smell invaded the bedroom. Finally, I too, drifted into a muddy dream of Anzio and German mortar shells.

During the long midnight a thunderous crash awakened us. At first I stamped it a rare nightmare, but Betsi's voice contradicted that theory. "Someone's broken into the house," she whispered. "They're in the patio!" Milliseconds later whirring wings flushed through the bedroom door and, as lights came on, Pedra perched on a thick dictionary, her glazed eyes staring uncertainly about her. Confused and weakened by the flight, she tightened her grip around the book, then teetered into unconsciousness. Betsi leaped from bed and caught her before she fell to the floor.

Momentarily we had not associated the crash with Pedra for once bedded she never left her comfort but, delirious, she did. Bewildered, she tumbled from bed and smashed into the patio window, plummeted to the floor, rose and instinctively boomeranged into our bedroom. There in a final desperate effort, she fluttered to the booklined wall and crash-landed. Her brilliantly clear message signaled how much she needed us, how much she wanted our companionship. Even in death.

Betsi brought a heating pad and her cardboard bed close to us. She fluffed corduroy comforters around the sick quail and tucked her in and Pedra managed a single delicate coo. Her closed eyes and quiet puffed feathers in semi-darkness created the illusion of a large bird. But Pedra was without substance and resistance for life diminished rapidly. Her tired body rose and fell with terrifying irregularity as the tiny trickle of life dripped away in the night.

Pedra's apparent death made me feel about as bad as I had ever felt including the loss of good Army buddies. About nine hundred men in my company F had died or were injured, including the Anzio five hundred, but somehow none seemed to cause the grief that Pedra did. I wanted to cry.

We increased vigilance, for she lay in bed still comatose. Next morning Betsi forced liquid antibiotics and vitamins every fifteen minutes, half a drop at a time. Her weight dropped alarmingly to almost half and we watched the scales scarcely tip a meager three ounces. She seemed weightless when we cleaned the bed. Formerly proud glossy feathers, which she had constantly preened and oiled throughout the day, now lay in a jumbled, dull and faded mass around her emaciated body. She had not preened since the respiratory virus imprisoned her energy. Nor did she care. Glazed eyes stared myopically at us, but she could neither rise nor shift her body. Her head tipped awkwardly to one side on the corduroy blanket as if excessively tired. Several times daily we thought she cooed softly, but were never certain.

Our slender hope strengthened gradually when she survived the second day, the third, and finally a blessed fourth, but ten days after Thanksgiving Pedra was still barely alive. Resembling an incubator baby more than a teenaged quail, she lay in bed only vaguely aware we existed. She seemed a great distance from us. She could not, or would not, eat solid food and, concerned about secondary infection, Betsi continued antibiotics. Without solids her weight drifted lower.

Imperceptibly Pedra improved, but still slept in our bedroom. We never passed her bed without speaking and one day she answered. The next day her eyes opened and Betsi offered a meal worm, a delicacy she normally savored. Pedra's head barely lifted, glanced indecisively at the wiggling morsel and drooped to the corduroy without opening her mouth.

"She should be thinking about the Junior prom instead of trying to survive," Betsi told me and, as always when Betsi's spirits plunged, mine followed, for Pedra still was an extremely sick girl.

She did improve. Convalescing slowly, one morning she tried to rise, but collapsed and lay gathering strength for another effort. She had eaten no solids for two weeks, although we tempted her daily with chopped broccoli, lettuce and meal worms.

Finally one morning, lying on one side, still not able to stand, she slowly pecked at a broccoli flowerlet. After three pecks, Pedra closed her eyes and rested, but she had eaten. "She's going to make it," I said with conviction.

That afternoon Pedra drank, unassisted, from her lid and pecked twice at parsley. At nightfall she inched to the bed's edge and peered over its lip, glancing at us with open inquisitive eyes. "She's well," I said.

"Not quite," Betsi cautioned. "The 'NO VISITOR'S' sign is still out."

Improvement continued each day. She staggered a few walking steps at first and timidly preened her wing feathers. Mainly she rested. When returned to her beloved kitchen bookshelf she grew noticeable stronger. By mid-December she balanced on one leg easily, devoured meal worms and preened non-stop.

Betsi's unbounded affection for the convalescent remained undiminished. No child ever received more serious devotion. If I smirked regarding her continuous attention to Pedra, she stared at me as though I possessed terminal idiot's disease. I soon learned to censor my thoughts even withholding comments when she chopped parsley, and offered the greenery to Pedra on a fingertip as though it was caviar.

One problem never mentioned during Pedra's illness was the rapid approach of Christmas. In addition to normal excitement, we expected a 10-day Marine invasion. They were a hardy lot. Enroute from Tennessee to a new station in

Hawaii, four Marines expected to land on our doorstep only days before the big holiday. Our daughter and son-in-law, both sergeants in the Corps, and children aged five and four, scheduled their arrival for alohas, Santa Claus and Pedra. Priorities remained indistinct, but Pedra perched high on their list.

We knew that Pedra might have handled the military encroachment easily if she were healthy, but the straggly three-ounce bag of bones and feathers seemed no contest now. Although we prayed for rapid improvement, only two short weeks remained. With an exceptional rapid recovery Pedra might have a chance.

Next morning Betsi woke with a scream. "Something's wrong with Pedra again!"

We listened briefly to an agonizing squawk in the kitchen and sprang from bed. In the morning light, mournful distress signals floated from Pedra's pulsating throat. She glanced sideways at us and strode back and forth inside her bed, obviously in pain. Then she hunched downward and cried. We never had heard her cry—no other word describes the sound—and continuous pleading wails for help flowed from her throat. If she had been a wolf baying at a full moon we would have understood. Then she sank into bed and lay quiet.

"She's sick again. Worse, this time." Betsi seemed to experience as much pain as Pedra. That morning Betsi waited at the pet store door for its opening and returned with more erythromycin. Force feeding commenced but Pedra did not respond to antibiotics. Betsi added aspirin to the formula. Meanwhile Pedra wailed continuously and circled her bed as though trying to walk away from pain. No simple illness had invaded her innards. She hurt badly and needed help. Betsi increased the aspirin. "She's got appendicitis, a violent toothache or she's having a baby," Betsi diagnosed.

"Couldn't be a toothache. Quail don't have 'em and she's too young to have babies."

"Then it's appendicitis," my bird-doctor wife diagnosed.

Complaints continued throughout the morning and at times she simply lifted her head, quail fashion, and howled. Her plume lay at half-mast. Erythromycin did not relieve her and she stalked, tiger like, in her bed. She refused food and finally hunkered in her box at lunchtime. By early afternoon, she quieted. Betsi provided erythromycin and fresh bedding at two o'clock and, lifting the fragile bird, a banshee shriek flooded the kitchen. I thought Betsi, too, had joined the wolf pack, for it was her voice. "Quick! Look! Pedra's laid an egg!" In the rumpled folded corduroy rested an egg, and not much larger than a sparrow's, (obviously the cause of her distress). Mainly beige but spattered with dark chocolate brown it was beautiful.

Her symptoms were not. Traumatic throes of egg production and laying decimated her entire system. Someplace a secret button pressed against her ovaries and an unwanted explosion occurred. She simply was too young to produce eggs. Not completely recuperated from her respiratory illness, egg production again placed Pedra on the critical list. Betsi labeled the kitchen an intensive-care area.

Pedra's stamina lessened with each egg. She barely walked. Her appetite disappeared again and she continually pleaded with us to subdue her pain. Betsi remembered half-grain codeine capsules left from an ancient surgery and prepared to mix them with erythromycin, but after the fourth egg in as many days she abandoned all home remedies and searched for professional help.

The bird veterinarian and Betsi bonded instantly through common sympathy for Pedra. Over the telephone the bird doctor said, "Some women and birds aren't cut out to have babies. They have problems."

"Oh," cried Betsi, who understood those things better than I did, "you mean like premenstrual syndrome?"

"Much worse than that. They die," the veterinarian counselled an already depressed Betsi who was not poised for defeat. Delving into her store of medical knowledge she probed further, "What about spaying? We don't need children. We only want Pedra! Can't that be done on birds?"

"Yes," came the reply. "Spaying can be performed, but odds are so great against survival we don't do it unless we want to sacrifice the bird."

"Spaying doesn't sound like a good solution," Betsi whispered as much to herself as to the veterinarian.

"It isn't. There's not much to be done. I'm sorry. It's a cross we ladies bear."

Betsi slowly put down the receiver and faced me, pale and defeated. "Pedra can't take much more," she said.

But cretin-sized devils armed with flaming pitchforks continued dancing in Pedra's innards, picking and searing her gut. The next day she laid a fifth egg, Siamese, and attached at the midline. The oversized mutant caused more than usual pain, but she rested quietly afterward as though marshalling strength for the next egg. In desperation Betsi called her bird doctor again. "Can't we do something? She's laying eggs two at a time, Siamese fashion."

The sympathetic doctor carefully explained we probably were responsible for Pedra's problem. Her egg-laying mechanism—normally triggered in spring—was detonated by a dietary abundance of vitamin A and increased light, a combination of factors found during spring mating. We had artificially, and prematurely, triggered nature's plan with continuous fresh broccoli, lettuce and spinach meals. Incandescent light accomplished the rest. In truth, Pedra's problem was our fault!

In parting the veterinarian continued, "Keep a sharp eye for yolk peritonitis," she warned. "It's part of premature laying syndrome. When birds produce too many yolks for the number of shells, yolks infiltrate the birds's system and yolk peritonitis results."

Betsi, already limp from too much knowledge, gasped. "What happens then?"

"They die. Yolk peritonitis is absolutely fatal to birds. There's no prevention and no cure. I'm truly sorry."

Betsi faced me slowly, then hovered over Pedra, praying for improved symptoms. Instead they worsened.

Daily eggs, carefully dated and labeled, shrank smaller each day with paper-thin shells. "At least the softer eggs don't cause her as much pain," I reasoned, "As long as it doesn't develop into yolk peritonitis."

Betsi stared with defiant eyes. "Don't mention those words!"

So severely did egg laying tax Pedra's strength she reminded us of a bird-like Toulouse-Lautrec. She scrambled painfully around the floor on her knees—for her legs could not support her—feebly pecking at imaginary food. She even refused ice cream. Her weight declined further and she slept most of the time. Spasmodically she awakened, shuddered and cried. Hourly, it seemed, her resistance for life diminished.

In the final days before Christmas we three seemed closer than ever despite her pain and impending death. Dark glazed eyes implored for help and she communicated with quiet thin chirps. Her voice deteriorated, too, and at times we barely heard her. In bed that night, as I dropped off, Pedra appeared, clear as a picture, a tiny hyperactive infant skittering across the slippery floor in the supermarket. Again, I watched with disbelief as Betsi scooped the chick up and closeted Pedra inside her blouse. Then, half awake, I heard myself promise, "When Pedra's gone we'll never have another bird. I couldn't stand it."

The next morning Betsi watched Pedra desperately try to stand, then topple over, her head dangling on the floor. Her debilitation, clearly marked by acute pain, lack of energy and complete disinterest in us, broke Betsi's heart. "If there's a God," she cried, finally coming to peace with herself, "He'll either take her from us or stop the eggs." 🐦

Chapter Thirteen

Without fanfare Pedra stopped laying. Her plaintive cries ceased and slowly an interest in broccoli and meal-worms redeveloped. During the first breakfast she tentatively pecked at a broccoli crumb, seemed to taste it thoughtfully, considering it with both her eyes and mouth before contemplating another bite. Deciding one nibble to be enough, she abandoned the remaining broccoli and sank into a meditative siesta.

That afternoon Betsi placed two mealworms in front of her. Pedra carefully evaluated the delicacy, shook her head as if telling us they were not fresh enough. "She's coming along," Betsi said. "At least she's looking at food."

It was a particularly desolate space in time for us despite Christmas plans. Pedra's pitiful body resembled a tiny, half-plucked pigeon. Frail and only three ounces compared to a strapping six ounces a month ago, she struggled without substance. Scrawny, unpreened feathers failed to cover ravages of her double tragedies. But she had survived. The long stumbling road to complete recovery lay ahead with Christmas only seven days away.

We prayed Pedra could survive the Marine obstacle course. Both sergeants could be controlled, but the grand-sergeants, aged four and five, offered massive bunkers of resistance. Five-year-old Brandy manned observation posts atop refrigerators and in top shelves of dark closets rather than settling in overstuffed chairs with cabbage patch dolls. She owned a green beret, a realistic toy submachine gun, and wore both as badges of honor.

Johnnie, at four, was banished from kindergarten before he started. He made family history. A rather tart official prohibited him from further education due to a dental problem. He had, the principal told his parents, compulsively bitten several classmates during indoctrination. A teacher ushered him home for remedial counseling so, even optimistically, Pedra faced severe problems.

The family cleared Tennessee camp driving west in two four-wheel drive pick-ups. Their estimated time of arrival, demanding intense travel, placed them on our doorstep three or four days before Christmas. We left Pedra briefly and bought a tree. Then, thinking about the Marine grandchildren, Betsi took several deep breaths and slowly exhaled. "This will be an interesting Christmas," she said.

Prior to Pedra's sickness she could have coped with the young Marines, but her fight-for-life banished all self-confidence. Sharp protesting squeaks warned us against stepping on her as we walked around, for she could not move quickly and we wondered how she would respond to eager, curious, but loving hands. "She has four days before facing front-line duty," Betsi said, counting days on her fingers.

"Think of it as 96 hours," I suggested. "It seems longer."

A Christmas whirlwind came over us and odors of spruce garlands, Oregon holly and mistletoe spread through the small condominium. Preparation of cookies and candy, fruitcakes and puddings occupied days and late evenings. In the excited tumble of preparation, we wondered how the hours had escaped.

Pedra humped disconsolately at our elbow, a vaguely interested convalescent. "Things always work out," Betsi said reading my mind. "She's gaining. I can see it. Every day she's better."

"At least we have one superb weapon on our side," I told Betsi.

"What?" she asked grasping for a straw of hope.

"Discipline! Everyone in the family is a Marine and the Corps is dedicated to discipline. That's the solution. Discipline." I hammered my fist on the table so hard a vase of flowers rattled to the floor and spread water and petals over the carpet. "We'll tell them Pedra's sick and ask them to leave her alone. There's no problem."

Betsi sprinkled spangles on sugar cookies, nodded and then, using her Gravel Gertie voice, said, "Discipline. You're right. Discipline and God." When she spoke in that tone I knew she didn't believe a single word I said.

In spite of ourselves Christmas spirit trapped us in a crack-the-whip mood and flung us into holiday orbit. All shapes and sizes of brightly colored boxes enveloped the Christmas tree and when light shone on the collected mysteries a spirit of excitement enmeshed us too. It was a sense of frolic not experienced since retirement. Even Pedra seemed happier.

She dust bathed daily in the garden, managing short energetic patio flights and spent hours preening disreputable feathers and repairing her ratty appearance. Eating habits improved and she devoured mealworms with gusto, even flying to the table for samples of cookie dough and freshly-baked bread. Most important, she communicated with me again. Not the garrulous, commanding conversations we previously had enjoyed, but long, quiet convalescent visits. Her curiosity in Christmas increased and she methodically examined the mountain of gifts beneath the tree. Clearly changes had been made and she approved.

Along with Christmas excitement we tackled Pedra's photosensitivity problem. If increased light triggered egg production, we determined to dramatically shorten the light she received. If artificial light—and our ignorance—had induced premature eggs, we intended to change that condition. Vowing she should never again know a midnight sun (incandescent or natural), Betsi cut a double-layered corduroy swatch and hung it in front of Pedra's bed.

She tucked the curtain under books on the shelf above Pedra's sleeping quarters. It made a perfect small dark room. In the morning I could raise and anchor the flap into the books above as Pedra walked out to my hand.

Our perfect theory caused us to wonder how Pedra would react. She always had enjoyed her penthouse bookshelf with its open vistas of the kitchen table while looking into the garden and across the desert. Would the blackout curtain remind her of early prison in the apple box? It certainly provided total midnight and met all our specifications. Success or failure depended on Pedra.

As usual, she surprised us. The first night she insisted on pulling the curtain herself. At bedtime she scratched the soft mattress vigorously and investigated for gremlins, turning several times and glancing into every corner. Then, to our utter amazement, she aggressively pecked at the curtain flap above her head. It soon fell into place and we gave her a standing ovation. If a wrinkle appeared she worked and smoothed it from the inside with rapid pecks until the corduroy hung flat. For the first time we suspected she might not be such a bird brain.

When we bragged about her performance, our friends scoffed. They came and watched. Predictably, every night, Pedra flew to bed about eight o'clock and immediately pulled her curtain. Usually it fell easily into place. If not, she smoothed the dropped cloth from the inside as carefully as if it were a contoured bedsheet. To be honest, when we knew curious visitors were coming we carefully positioned the hanging corduroy so that it would fall in place—much like the trigger of a simple box trap. Pedra did the rest.

Once the curtain was satisfactorily neat, Pedra relaxed and lost herself in preening and soft cooing. We heard her stretch and manicure long wing feathers, reaching into her preening gland at the tip of her spine and extracting minuscule drops of oil then carefully smoothing the lubricant into each feather. Her bedtime toilet rivalled the prissiest courtesan.

After the nest quieted (since she did not relish disturbances during preening), Betsi raised the corduroy and tempted her with a nightcap of broccoli and warm water. Pedra accepted small portions, for she didn't believe in heavy eating before sleep. Then she settled comfortably into her blanket and slept until after daylight. One time I chided Betsi for the special love she heaped on the recuperating bird, but she told me, "It takes more than medicine to cure. Tender loving care might be the most important element." Then she suddenly added, "You know, quail are human, too."

Our lengthy Christmas gift list diminished daily and we turned to housekeeping with high spirits since Pedra's health dramatically improved. Two projects faced us: garage cleaning (for both of us despised that chore and chronically ignored it) and manicuring the garden. The second chore included elimination of a friendly black-widow spider, a long-term tenant housed beneath the barbecue pit. Pedra helped inside the garage, chatting and preening from atop a folding ladder. She seemed, except for her spectacularly disreputable appearance, nearly well. Even garage cleaning proved easy with Pedra's help.

Outside, the dormant fig tree presented no problem, for its broad hand-like leaves had long ago blown into the desert. The pineapple guava and ornamental pomegranate were quickly pruned as well as both mints, still flourishing in December. Pedra watched as a sidewalk supervisor while we trimmed. The pineapple sage with bright red blossoms shrank from our pruning shears, but Pedra did not care, for it meant nothing to her. For some reason it was the single plant in the entire garden she ignored. We cherished it principally for hummingbirds who enjoyed the blossoms. Thorough raking and mulching produced a near professional effect and we looked with pleasure on it. "Now for madame spider," I said.

Hourglass V, fifth generation black widow in our home, wallowed in comfortable secluded quarters two feet from the glassed patio under the barbecue smoker. She spun a tangle of uncommonly strong webbing in the space between the drip pan and bottom container. We allowed her free lodging for two reasons. First, she owned squatter's rights since her ancestors had homesteaded the desert long before we invaded and she was a compatible tenant. We seldom saw her during daylight, but she sometimes joined us on the outside patio after the sun disappeared. Secondly, she provided our hummingbirds a perpetual supply of nesting material. We shamefully bribed the tiny scatter-flighted birds with abundant pineapple sage, ornamental pomegranate blossoms and flowering herbs, for we enjoyed watching hummers beyond normal reason.

If hummers enjoyed our flowers year round they were magnetized during nesting season by the black widow's nest. The deadly spider produced possibly the strongest and softest of all webs. During mating, hummers flew practically nonstop to the barbecue and no matter the destruction, the faithful widow frantically repaired and replenished webbing around the clock. We considered her an ideal tenant.

More than one surprised guest, seated in the garden sipping Scotch whisky, gasped in astonishment when Rufus hummers whipped between their legs enroute to the barbecue, for hummers flew in surprisingly direct lines to their targets. Seconds later, with nesting fuzz stringing from their beak, they zipped back through our guest's legs, tickling flesh and rippling pants in a wake of whirling wings and gossamer webbing. Thank-you notes from departed guests many times failed to recall Grand Canyon trips, beef Wellington and Crown Royal, but they never forgot hummingbirds' flights between their legs. Never.

Hourglass V's lease did not expire, normally, at Christmas. We served eviction notice when her own nesting urge struck. At first appearance of the large white egg sac we promptly destroyed her and the sac, for she was a persistent mother. If we only destroyed the sac, she promptly fashioned another. We did not relish baby sitting two hundred black widow infants.

The grandchildren's arrival that night, however, dictated an early holiday death for, discipline or not, their curiosity about the deadly insect only a child's arm's length away might prove too tempting. Reluctantly we advanced the execution date.

Killing black widows is about as easy as assassinating a colony of cobras. They seldom cooperated enough to lie on a hard surface until we stomped them to death. And good sportsmanship on our part postponed her demise when she joined us at sunset during social hour. It would have been a sellout of her confidence in us.

Spiders are also among the most resilient creatures. When we surprised one and stomped her fiercely we later discovered she had completely recovered without apparent damage. Insecticides did not always work, either. Heavy blasts of all known poisons curled and shriveled them beyond apparent survival. They melted into insignificant balls and lay stone quiet. We learned to beware of those actors. They quickly survived and returned home to increased egg production. Even an insecticide hangover failed to deter them once the reproductive urge struck and they merrily repaired their fortress and built another egg sac within a day.

We did use insecticides as tranquilizers so Betsi, myself and Pedra, who tagged at our heels, strolled to the barbecue pit armed with the deathbomb. Tactics required a direct hit with the spray to stun and render her temporarily harmless, then quickly extricating the spider from the web, we thoroughly stomped her on the sidewalk. We had successfully killed many black widows in that fashion.

The brilliant red and black hourglass glistened in the web's centerfold and I tipped the barbecue toward the white wall, completely exposing her. She faced me defensively and I blasted a splash of poison into her face. She dropped, curled and fell half an inch into her web. "She's cooperating beautifully," I said. "There's no problem."

So swiftly that we talked about it for months, Pedra stepped forward and pecked. The widow attacked with furious speed, poisoning Pedra someplace along her neck. Startled, Pedra staggered backward and nearly fell. The weight of her head became too great and she slumped awkwardly and quietly to the sidewalk. Neither of us remembered destroying the widow. The spider's remains lay splashed beyond recognition on the sidewalk, the entire insecticide can empty. Our planned murder had been a split second too late. Like lost cousins, Pedra and trouble had found each other again. 🐦

Chapter Fourteen

To quell the panic in her heart, Betsi cried long, wailing sobs and cradled the poisoned quail close to her heart. She placed her bird in the table box watching helplessly as Pedra's eyes drooped nearly closed. Slowly Pedra tried rising, but collapsed in a feathery heap, helpless. Pressing both feet into the sand, she half rose then dropped again. A quizzical expression seemed to spread over her face as though attempting to explain she had only tried to help us. Clearly she did not understand why her legs didn't function. Then her head violently twitched upward, her wing feathers jerked in rapid spasms and quite helplessly we watched her entire body convulse.

"She's dying," Betsi cried. "That damned spider!'

"Not quite. Black widow bites aren't always fatal," I heard myself saying without conviction, for I knew the potency of black widow venom. In our shocked condition a thousand carillons seemed to explode in the kitchen, but it was only the telephone. "Hey mom, guess who?"

Our daughter, enroute to us, explained that a slashing Texas ground blizzard had grounded them, knee deep in snow. They would not arrive tonight. "We figured Sun City a three-day drive, mom, but weather changed our minds. I'm as disappointed as you. I wish we were there right now. We need some cheering up."

Numbly Betsi listened as her daughter continued. "We still have two days before Christmas and we'll see you and Santa even if we have to come on a sleigh. We'll be there. That's a Marine promise." Johna described the harrowing blizzard, but her voice finally slowed. "Is everything all right mom? You seem so far away."

"Everything's fine. Drive carefully. We'll be waiting for you." Betsi hung the telephone limply on the wall. "I think I'll get drunk."

"You don't drink," I reminded her.

"I forgot." She moaned, sinking beside the paralyzed bird stretched full length in her warm box. Betsi massaged Pedra and her hand drifted to the quail's feet. "Her feet are so cold. They shouldn't be cold," she cried.

"No, they shouldn't be cold," I repeated.

Even the house seemed unhappy and a brooding atmosphere of tragedy infected the kitchen despite twinkling Christmas lights and merry carols. "Turn off those lights," Betsi shouted in frustration. "And the radio too. I'm sick of that *God Rest You Merry Gentlemen* junk!" I thought she would scream or smash her teacup against the table before she quieted. "This will be the worst Christmas ever." Tears dripped slowly down her cheeks and she continued staring at Pedra.

Pedra did not argue. Stashed in her high bookshelf, she watched us with puzzled eyes, her left side completely paralyzed. She seemed only vaguely interested in her disability, but periodically tried to rise in noisy, disoriented flutters as if the next attempt would be successful. However the left leg could sustain no weight and her wings could not steer. She sat in bed waiting for a miracle. Finally her eyes closed and to blot her pathetic condition from us, we lowered her corduroy curtain.

Strangely, in bed we had nothing to say to each other. Usually we talked over daily happenings and pooled small optimisms, but tonight none surfaced as we tumbled and thrashed on the great double bed, seeking solace in troubled sleep. I finally dozed away praying for a quick and happier tomorrow.

Betsi checked the invalid hourly until five o'clock when I arose. She slept fitfully, mumbling strange syllables into the pillow, her hair tumbling around her arms and face in frightful disarray. In the dark I groped instinctively through the patio, automatically searching in Pedra's bed while reaching for the light switch. Pedra was gone! Startled, I snaked fingers through the corduroy curtain and fumbled inside the cold box. No question. She was not there! Stifling a cry I switched the light on to examine shelves where she sometimes crawled and waited. Paralyzed, she could not have flown, but glancing to the floor I saw her.

Pedra stretched full length on cold kitchen tile. Touching her icy stiff body, my stomach contracted and fierce sharp pains stabbed my throat. "God," I thought, "she's really dead this time." Instinctively I shouted, "Betsi come quickly!"

Tenderly we wrapped the cold rigid body inside a woolen coverlet and laid her on the heating pad. Even the warm bright lamp overhead failed to reassure us, for she lay oblivious to our presence. Betsi massaged Pedra's feathers and feet. "She's breathing," she said. "I can feel her breathing." Pedra's fluffy body heaved gently, her eyelids opened downward (unlike humans, quail shut their eyes in a single upward motion) and rested, staring at us briefly before sealing them softly shut.

We reconstructed the accident. She had crawled to the lip of her bed and fallen five feet to the sharp corner of a step stool. "The fall should have killed her," Betsi said.

"It did," I thought. "Wait."

Betsi's nerves dictated silence. Whatever I said might have reduced her to jelly, so I remained quiet. Our tolerance for Christmas ho-ho-ho's vanished and even the radio was still. "We should have known," Betsi wailed to me. "We should have brought her to our bed. She tried to get to us. We simply weren't there to help when she needed us most." And tears flowed again.

I mentally wrote off our small crippled friend, realizing the advantage of her leaving us before the children arrived. Easier for us, too. But terrified with Pedra's death summons, Betsi tried to brush away the smell of doom in the house by dragging herself to the stove and pouring hot tea. Afterward she sat, staring into the garden, massaging encouragement and circulation into Pedra's frail body.

I made hasty funeral arrangements. "We'll bury her under the savory. She liked that best."

"Not yet," Betsi replied. Together we listened to the gentle hissing teakettle as morning drifted into afternoon. Betsi continued massaging her emaciated friend.

"I really never wanted more children," Betsi said, the pallor of her face reflecting the death in her hands.

I watched in horrified fascination how my wife might appear at eighty or ninety years. Thin, pinched and frightened. Maybe even toothless and balding, for her mother had been nearly bald before a brain tumor destroyed her reason and a prep nurse had finished the job by shaving her head glistening pink. "Betsi," I mused to myself, "is not the only person near the breaking point."

125

Pedra opened her trusting eyes at three o'clock. She took no food, nor did she stir. Only her eyes followed us gravely and her head hung limply on the bed. Later she tried moving. It was then we discovered she could not control her head. "She's broken her neck," Betsi moaned. "I broke mine in high school and she acts the same way."

Quail own more neck bones than a giraffe and one or two small bones could easily break or dislocate during a fall. We had observed numerous birds fracture necks or bash skulls while diving into our patio windows. Sometimes they died. We buried them among flowers and herbs and the garden developed into a crowded bird cemetery. We would not relish the latest addition.

"Let's hope she was lucky," I said.

Betsi continued stroking her bird with long soft caresses, barely skimming Pedra's feathers in her desire to transmit curative effects through love and prayer. "The worst is over. Nothing more can happen. God, that's a blessing," she added.

Late evening, while adjusting her bed we discovered more damage. Her left rib cage indicated severe compressed fractures. Careful manipulation revealed a depression as large as a teaspoon. We speculated she might have several fractured ribs and internal bleeding. "If she lives through the night she owns every right to survive. Christmas owes her that much," Betsi said.

During the next five minutes I contemplated Pedra's crushed rib cage, that delicate formation of bones so casually cast aside while eating roasted quail. Nearly without substance, they nevertheless performed miraculous duty for the duration of life, except when abused. Pedra, nearly comatose, had fallen dead weight to the floor, splintering her ribs. She could not have ruptured a major blood vessel or she would already be dead. Maybe that was the Christmas miracle for which we'd asked. Her future seemed in the hands of God. In a moment of self-pity I wondered where we had gone astray. We'd never had such problems with our other children and in general frustration and despair I slammed my fist on the table nearly breaking two small bones in my wrist.

Yet, watching her closely, I came to understand the narrowing gap between us. No chasm of misunderstanding ever existed for Pedra, but for me she had only been a quail and a troublesome one at that. Now, instinctively, I reached across and pressed my hands in healing fashion over her unhappy feathers. During the months she had quietly and patiently entered my heart without a ripple. I would miss her. That night we never left her side. Her kitchen bed, temporarily highboarded with books and cardboard, prevented escape. We worried unnecessarily. Pedra could not move.

She roused us on the morning of Christmas eve with sharp chirps and waited for breakfast on two wobbly legs. Devouring three meal worms, half a broccoli flowerlet and warm water, she apparently enjoyed food for the first time since spider venom poisoning. But she could not walk!

By early afternoon she staggered in tight circles on the carpet, forever in danger of falling on her head with each step. Partial paralysis claimed her left side and she limped three erratic steps before landing on her beak. Fifteen minutes later with renewed energy she rose and aimed at us, but careened off like a slow shooting star. Her body and brain simply spoke different languages.

Rib fractures tilted her more off balance and she drifted to the floor after only a minute. She could not manipulate her head (supporting our broken neck theory) but throughout the afternoon, in crazy zigzag fashion, she attempted to reach us. In a couple of hours she lay at our feet, frustrated and exhausted. We understood. So were we.

Pedra certainly presented a strange sight. Scrawny and unkempt, her head canted sideways, her legs struggled to rise. Then she limped in odd directions as though lost in the dark. She managed at most three desperate steps, then collapsed in a feathery heap. Under different circumstances we might have suspected she had tippled too much Christmas cheer.

The Marines landed at 2010 hours which, in Sun City language, was ten minutes after eight o'clock. Both children, after fourteen grueling hours on icy roads, seemed tired but exhilarated. Their festive spirit punched holes through despondency and our spirits rose. Hot punch, cold beer and smoked turkey settled nerves as we readied for Christmas under the tree. Pedra crouched at my feet, nibbling small pieces of plum pudding. She adored suet.

Enhanced with the addition of Marine gifts, mysterious boxes nearly filled the corner, but their bulk proved no obstacle. Children's joy and enthusiasm reduced the mountain to a mass of wrinkled paper, ribbon and discarded boxes within an hour. Pedra watched the excitement with quiet interest before we placed her on a heating pad and gossiped until after midnight.

Suddenly the room quieted, our juices slowed as if a main valve had been turned off and a great fatigue pressed over us. For the first time Christmas carols filtered into our conscious.. Slow and melodic, *Silent Night* filled the house and Brandy, eyes numb with weariness, mumbled, "They don't know the words." The carol, sung by a French children's choir, so sweetly characteristic of Christmas, brought tears to our eyes. "It's French. French children are singing for us," I told her.

"Is it Christmas in French, too?" Brandy asked.

"Yes. It's Christmas everywhere."

"I'm glad," she said. "Because I like Christmas," and she plunged into powerful sleep in Betsi's arms. I carried Johnnie and laid him among his presents. We extinguished lights, leaving only flickering red votive candles casting shadows on a bower of red poinsettias against the wall.

Pedra lay, open-eyed in her bed beside us, neither moving nor communicating. "This wasn't the worst Christmas, was it?" I asked Betsi while securing night latches.

She smiled through tired lips. "Oh no. It's a wonderful Christmas. The kids are safe, Pedra's alive and its Christmas everywhere."

Hot air balloon rides, desert picnics, picking fresh oranges and cotton filled vacation days. All too soon we called goodbyes, Happy New Years and waved alohas to the Hawaii-bound Marines. Both children had been admirable. Anticipated problems had not surfaced and their departure left us with a giant void that only a crippled quail could fill.

Slowly Pedra recuperated. Her bright black eyes focused on us, yet her body steered other courses. Desperately she flew short bursts directly in our direction, crash-landed, canted fearfully away, then reoriented in a circle of half-steps and flew toward us again. By repetition and luck she finally arrived exhausted at our feet. Her efforts reminded us of a stammering friend who, frantically searched for a simple word, but could not find it. How we wanted to pick her up and deposit her at our feet! It could have been done so easily, yet she rejected our help and continued the heartbreaking trip to recovery.

She rated a solid ten for determination. Her unfailing courage never faltered. Week after week she improved. Her walking circles grew larger and finally we watched a 10-foot flight across the patio. Her stiff neck remained and she could not preen. Her left leg functioned sparingly and, lying in bed she scratched her head softly with a large toe. She still could not stand for long periods and we despaired of seeing her walk normally or preen again. Dull, grubby feathers prompted Betsi to brush and wipe them with light mineral oil.

Despite Betsi's beautifying efforts Pedra's appearance deteriorated. Her neck jutted at an odd angle, giving the impression of constantly reading over someone's shoulder. She could only turn her head a degree or two. Her landing gear remained faulty and she tumbled over the floor after the briefest flight. In addition we thought she had started to molt. Stray feathers floated about the house and she appeared shabbier than before.

Late February she twisted her neck and preened a single wing feather. Daily we observed steadier progress and one afternoon she reached into her breast and discarded a worn feather. That milestone achievement marked the beginning of rapid progress. We rose and cheered the morning she reached her preening gland near her tail. She extracted a tiny speck of wax and oiled a long flight feather then glanced sideways at us to see if we had witnessed her accomplishment. For her it was a monumental achievement! Round the clock she preened. When I raised her morning curtain she sat busily stroking feathers. She preened during meals, seemingly compelled to pause between broccoli or parsley and clean a feather she had been thinking about.

Nightmares started again. We had missed the sudden single cries in the night not heard since November. Now they recommenced. Lone, frightening cries in the darkness awakened us and we smiled. Pedra was returning to normal.

Her devotion to me intensified. I kept a sharp vigil while walking for fear of stepping on her so closely did she shadow me. If I left the room, she cried long wailing sobs then immediately stopped when I returned, greeting me with happy homecoming clucks. Daily naps began again. I realized her longing for naps with me when she started waiting for me on the bed immediately following lunch. Betsi cut several large corduroy patches for my chest, Pedra leaped aboard, scratched the material, settled under my chin and slept, her feathers tickling my throat. I normally didn't sleep on my back, but quickly learned to do so, for Pedra did not want to sleep sidesaddle. She jumped off if I turned sideways, striding along my side, clucking mild objections until I turned again on my back. A mixture of love and loyalty pumped through her heart and, looking fixedly into my eyes, she chirped quiet thank you. Through no effort of mine we became inseparable companions.

She also enjoyed typing. When I moved to the typewriter she immediately joined me atop the carriage, chirping encouragement. Riding the carriage platen like a bareback bronc rider, she snorted short exclamations each time the carriage returned. Other times she investigated the electric keyboard, resulting in blotched messages that made, according to Betsi, more sense than my typing. Eventually tiring of the machine, she hopped to the floor and rested between my feet. She paid little attention to Betsi, neither visiting nor acknowledging her. How many times did her mind remember the clean beds, fresh food, loving care that Betsi heaped on her? Not once!

By late March, three months after her series of accidents, a new strength filtered through her blood and she tucked her head behind her wing when she slept. After the first time, she instantly withdrew it and faced us with an unwinking gaze as if to say, "You didn't think I could do it, did you?" And Betsi said, "No, you varmint, we didn't," and a great happiness filled her heart despite Pedra's reluctance to communicate with her.

Pedra immediately repeated her feat to prove it was no accident, cooing with self satisfaction. In truth, she had not been capable of such pleasure for many months. Her left rib cage remained appallingly depressed and she struggled with a gimpy left leg, so we realized she would never walk or fly as well as before. No matter, our Pedra was alive!

The perfume of hot, yeasty whole wheat bread, green chili stew and homemade pure vanilla ice cream filtered through the house. A fresh, massive garlic string hung temptingly over the refrigerator and, in the herb garden, the chatter of jolly, noisy finches filled the backyard with bird gossip. The golden sunshine of spring had returned and with it promises for a rosy future.

Clear headed with Pedra's recovery and in a burst of energy, we planned spring cleaning and decorating. That procedure six months ago would have been disastrous, but Pedra's elimination habits were no longer a problem. Major potty stops included the red Christmas cloth and the garden, which was flourishing with a continuous supply of fresh nitrogen. She also deposited droppings on my corduroy patches when I napped. Pedra was about as housebroken as she could be, so we determined it was time to redecorate and buy new furniture. That delayed step had been contemplated before Pedra arrived.

Painting, furniture shopping and carpet cleaning destroyed March and Pedra observed the entire upheaval with interest. Finally the painters disappeared. Clean carpets glistened and even the new patio furniture pleased Betsi so much she never once suggested changes. At last the comfortable condominium crackled with smugness and optimism. We were ready, after four months of upheaval, to a welcome retirement tranquility. Indeed, time had come to sort our dreams again and settle into rocking chairs. ➤

Chapter Fifteen

On April first I basked in the satisfaction of a job well done and settled in the patio overstuffed chair reading *Zorba the Greek*. The entire blissful day had drifted away and a mellowness settled over me after an afternoon nap and refreshing shower. Pedra stretched between my feet like a faithful collie, basking in soft spring sunlight. Previously she had jumped on my lap, examined the book and finding it slow reading, had nipped a couple of saw-toothed bites from the pages and perched on my shoulder. A quick step to the top of the large yellow chair elevated her and she stood surveying the garden for stray finches, which she regarded as interlopers. She remained there ten minutes, quite silent, then, convinced all was well in the garden, stepped on my shoulder, scooted over my belly, down to my knees, and finally dropped at my feet. The path was her normal staircase. Then she relaxed on the carpet, eyes blissfully closed, happy and healthy. Betsi entered the kitchen through the garage and interrupted my reverie. "I've got us a new baby." She grinned, nearly exploding with happiness.

I recognized the pixie smile. It was familiar. Her mother one day showed me a faded snapshot of Betsi swathed in a cast from her hips to her mandible, grinning through the white plaster—the result of a broken neck following an ill-advised dive into a shallow pool—and smirking as she did now. Her smile admitted an idiot's act, a look I had frequently seen on Pedra's face, but challenged objection. Still I did not believe her. On All Fool's day Betsi was not beneath exercising a joke at my expense.

"April fool to you, too," I said but she responded by poking a familiar net-covered shoe box into my face. Adjusting my trifocals I searched through the netting. Huddled in the darkest corner lay a miserable Gambel's quail about the size of a small peanut. Betsi had not been joking.

She pushed the box toward me, but I rejected it with both hands as though it contained a quart of AIDS virus. Blood rushed to my head and my ears rang like the anvil chorus score. I felt as if someone had poleaxed me. Betsi's sense of humor wore thin at times and I tried to smile, but failed. Incoherent with frustration I sputtered, "We've just redecorated and cleaned! How?..Why?..Where..?"

Overflowing with motherly love, she did not notice my near-coronary status and continued enthusiastically, "Don't blame me. It was an abandoned chick. It had no father" (a likely miracle, I thought) "and was runt of the litter. Mother couldn't take care of thirteen. Brothers and sisters killing it. Pecking order you know." Her rambling smoke-screen description didn't fool me. I recognized her technique. "Look!" she said to involve me in the fiasco, "it can hardly move."

My mind did not dwell on the quail's athletic prowess. Someone, somewhere, hated me! "Who did this to us?"

"Friends. Friends called me." She said and raised the net to assure herself the baby had not escaped.

"They are not friends," I shouted. "We don't need another quail. We've just finished redecorating. We're going to China..." I listed six more sensible reasons for not accepting another bird and Betsi responded with her usual logic.

"Don't be such an old poop," she said, "you'll love Pablito."

"Pablito?"

"Of course. Little Pablo. He's a boy quail. Pedra needs a baby brother or even a lover later on...and I need a son." Betsi fantasized lovers and big brothers while watching a squeaking chick squirm helplessly in the corner. Realistically I saw an incubator baby, special tutors and later on, mental health problems, for clearly Pablito was a throwback. A retard. His mother knew best when she and the family rejected him. But Betsi's gentle diplomatic pressures succeeded all too often and I prepared my defense carefully.

Fleeting thoughts of two birds, one a fine companion for the other, confused my mind but, finally common sense overwhelmed me. "No!" I shouted, "Listen to me. No!"

In the face of defeat, Betsi sensed victory and she blandly admitted it. "You don't mean it. You always say the strangest things at times like these." She leaned over the shoe box and spoke to Pablito. "He doesn't mean what he says. He really wants you." Pablito didn't answer, but shrank farther into the corner, compressing a tiny head into his beige body so he resembled a fuzzy, deformed nut.

All day I fought with every fiber against the lunacy of owning another bird, but at sunset my resistance weakened and I began to see the value of a larger family. Definite challenges faced us. Many friends ridiculed our adoption of Pedra. Others projected failure. So far we had been fortunate. Despite her setbacks she was alive, thanks totally to Betsi's loving care. But was Pedra an exception? Had we only been lucky? Alive, Pablito might provide answers. Dead, we'd never know. I tossed the coin of reason into the garbage, drank a double scotch and decided to keep him a day or two.

Acute maternal fever raged in Betsi's breast, her eyes glowed with intense love, and she nursed Pablito nonstop. Creating new formulas, she eye-droppered warm water into his craw and thrust soluble vitamins and prophylactic anti-biotics into his beak. She dared him to die.

After six days Pablito had not gained a dram. Indeed, his birthing weight was hardly reestablished. Although it is not uncommon for babies to lose weight shortly after birth, Pablito had not much to lose. Even with a full craw he barely tipped the quarter-ounce balance. Betsi's return for her time and money did not discourage her. He would develop, she reasoned.

Pablito was not an elegant chick. Matted fuzz and rickety legs suggested a long-term skid row residency and I told no one that he lived with us. If I had, Betsi would have earned full credit. Tiny pin feathers pushed through wing tips and he teetered as he walked, balancing like a tightrope walker challenging the Grand Canyon. Compared to other active chicks in the courtyard, Pablito clearly was a retard, for Gambel's chicks could scamper with lightning speed only minutes after hatching. But his vocal chords had not been impaired and he cheeped loudly and continuously. Betsi cherished his life like gold while I would have sold it for a copper.

During the second week he exploded into a hyperactive hell-raiser. No matter how observantly we had watched his development his instant change caught us unaware. Without warning he raced up the feather duster handle one morning, leaped to the patio in a fuzzy heap and disappeared.

Outside the box his voice seemed to have instantly failed although he had chattered at full volume only seconds ago. Dead quiet settled inside the patio and we searched an hour while he lay concealed under our feet. He discovered impossible hiding places. Simple house shadows and complete immobility rendered him nearly invisible. Pablito faded into books or magazines so easily we wondered if his father might have been a chameleon.

Once over the cardboard wall he could move three inches and vanish. The devil himself couldn't have found him. After four days of frustrating hunts—he seemed to enjoy the game—I told Betsi, "Get rid of that damned magician. I won't have him in the house."

Betsi's patience proved exasperating. "His health is better. We'll find a new home for him in a few days," she said, but as his cover and concealment game improved our search and rescue tactics crumbled.

We wondered about Pedra's acceptance of the baby. She ignored him! His interminable cheeping never aroused her curiosity, for they apparently spoke different languages. Since Pablito lived in his box except during feeding time the two never met. Sometime during Pablito's second week of rejuvenation he scampered up the feather duster, scratched a hole in the net, leaped through and fell eighteen inches on his head. He rebounded without pausing, feet spinning, spied Pedra and without a second's hesitation raced toward her.

Pedra was eating shelled walnuts in the sunny patio and casually glanced up as the whirling dervish exploded under her feathers. Pablito charged through her legs, nestled comfortably under her breast and issued small happy cheeps. Pedra was startled at the unexpected attention and uttered a series of surprised yelps. Then she stepped away from the intruder, glanced at the chick with what we later diagnosed as a sneer and sprang rapidly away from the irritant, reaching back only to peck Pablito stoutly on the head.

He blinked and raced to his nearest haven—Pedra's breast. Pedra moved and Pablito followed, for he had taken a liking to his sister. Still only mildly irritated, Pedra kicked at the nuisance under her skirt and, as anger rose, she pecked again and again as though a colony of fire ants had homesteaded her bosom. Pablito nimbly avoided all attacks and settled comfortably near her warm heart. When she dodged away he flowed spryly under his sister with the grace of an adagio dancer. Pedra was not amused.

She decided to ignore him and continued to peck at walnuts on the floor. After a few bites Pablito's curiosity conquered him and he darted four quick steps forward amongst breast feathers and dared to nibble Pedra's walnuts. The insult overwhelmed her and she nipped viciously at the baby, then flew to the couch and chirped loudly to herself. A snake had entered her garden of Eden.

Curiosity regarding pecking order always intrigued us and we possessed a chance to closely monitor that phenomenon. Pedra quickly indicated she would tolerate no infringement of her territory and wasted no time indoctrinating her half-ounce brother regarding his rights, which apparently did not exist. During Pedra's illnesses she had violently protected her territory from the grandchildren. Weak as a kitten she pecked their shoes and protested all love demonstrations aimed in my direction. When Brandy or Johnnie hugged and kissed me Pedra struggled closely to my toes and pecked unevenly at their shoes. Now healthy, she readied a no-nonsense defense of her rights.

Pablito, on the other hand, wasted no time declaring his love for Pedra. He discovered methods of escape from his cardboard box during the day and instantly flew to Pedra's wing and burrowed inside the living feather duster. There he cosied up warm and, hopefully secure, because except for the psychedelic feather duster he had no known relative. Except for Betsi, he was an unwanted orphan.

Pedra tried ignoring him. She faced a nearly impossible situation. If she basked in the sunshine, Pablito streaked across the carpet and nudged under the soft feathers, peeking out impudently as though he had stolen a cookie. At first Pedra jostled a bit and ignored the intrusion, but Pablito did not remain passive. He nudged, thrust and wiggled under Pedra's feathery canopy until she arose with dignity and stalked under the coffee table, settled down looking suspiciously around for gremlins. Pablito followed.

Tiny flapping wing stubs assisted his race toward Pedra. He streaked across the room and entered under her belly from the rear then, tickling through her breast, poked a cheerful head outside. Pedra was not happy and pecked viciously as though at a flea on a pogo stick, but she seldom struck her target once he gained entrance to her body, for Pablito was greased lightning. After several pecking failures Pedra flew shrieking to my knee and, as I cuddled her, she trembled violently.

A truce of sorts blossomed at mealtime. Pablito could not, or would not, eat from a dish, even rejecting food smeared on mirrors. He preferred eating from a small ice cream spoon with Betsi's help. Placing basic formula high on his preferred list he smacked his beak with gusto at its appearance although Pedra had long rejected baby formula for roast beef, buttered carrots and ice cream.

She refused formula until Pablito arrived, then her attitude changed. When Betsi removed formula from the refrigerator Pedra flew to the table and watched Pablito eat. After a few nibbling bites she could tolerate no more and, nearly walking over Pablito, stretched her neck across his shoulder and ate from the spoon, too.

We noticed other dietary changes. During infancy Pedra adored cut sunflower seeds (she couldn't eat the entire seed), and ate them until her craw bulged. One day she refused a single bite. We checked for rancidity, bought fresh seeds, and tried different brands. Still Pedra refused. We freezer-stored them and did not offer her any more. One morning Betsi removed the frozen seeds, chopped them, and Pedra raced across the room, for she was a magnificent sprinter. She hopped to the table, placed a large foot firmly upon the box and ate voraciously. Pablito, scrambling under her belly, claimed his share, too. So Pedra tolerated her brother— barely—at mealtime.

We analyzed her renewed interest in quail formula. Was it sincere or did she leap at the food only to claim a share she had previously rejected? Maybe. Was she jealous of Pablito's love for sunflowers seeds? Perhaps. Was she capable of jealousy? Positive answers never surfaced, for Pedra did not say. She continued eating peacefully with the baby and we welcomed her attitude change even if it lasted only a few minutes at the table.

Pedra placed broccoli flowerlets on the highest culinary pedestal. The sight of fresh or cooked broccoli set her flying to the kitchen counter. She ate not only flowerlets but the entire stalk. Pablito's appearance altered her consumption,

for she no longer enjoyed sole broccoli rights. Her little brother developed an instant craving bordering on addiction. When broccoli appeared so did Pablito, fluttering, scratching and scrambling for his share. Did he eat because Pedra wanted it? Conceivably. Or did he eat it out of pure orneriness? We judged that reason the best possibility for Pablito, even in infancy, was a different kind of bird.

As peacekeeper in the bird family Betsi built a broccoli jig with a spring-type clothes pin. It sat three inches above the table and held a perpetual (thanks to Betsi's munificence) supply of broccoli. Pedra reached it easily. Pablito could not. He stretched barely two inches on unstable feet. Leaping frantically upward for a bite he tipped backwards then fell awkwardly into Pedra's breast.

Pedra towered over the stripling, but Pablito was not easily denied and leaped again, fixing his beak into a stalk. His feet slipped and he fell into Pedra again. Pedra browsed above him dropping—quite unintentionally—tender tidbits from her beak. Pablito snapped at the freshly cut morsels as though they were newly hatched mosquitoes, catching some before they reached the table. He quickly cleaned every bite. The result was a marvelous synergistic banquet. Neither raised a voice, except in praise, during mealtime, and the sound of contented coos radiated throughout the kitchen. Betsi led the chorus.

Betsi never attempted to wean them from broccoli although she substituted parsley, Boston bibb lettuce and spinach for variety. They ate everything in complete harmony. If their limited vegetable diet caused colic we did not know, and if an overabundance of broccoli (they ate it three times daily) ruffled their innards, quick healing ensued and they returned again and again to broccoli. Vegetable heaven, in the guise of a broccoli jig, had arrived.

So Pablito grew. And grew. And grew. Male markings appeared more distinct daily and, although repeatedly warned that we could not distinguish sex this early, Pablito's dark, almost black facial fuzz, pronounced him a male in our opinion. Pedra never appeared so dark. His small heavy plume, prancing gaily over a tiny head, quickly established itself and we regarded this sign further evidence of manhood.

Betsi wanted a son! She rationalized a male would attach himself to her in the same manner that Pedra had imprinted on me. The only missing piece of sexual confirmation was Pedra's insistence on pecking his brains out. We had been told that Gambel's quail exhibited the highest respect for the opposite sex, but Pedra paid no attention to the dictate and walloped him continuously. Pablito didn't care. He was too busy growing up.

Although Pablito raced around the house during the day we double-locked him in at night. Mosquito netting and a sturdy beach towel established maximum security. It also reduced his astonishing escape rate. He ruined our day when, arising, we discovered an empty apple box. Frenzied searching began, often from daylight to breakfast, and we considered belling him, for he celebrated his triumphant absences in complete silence. Never far away but always invisible, he remained irritatingly mute. Even broccoli failed to lure him from concealment, for we suspected he recognized the trap. Other times, inside the apple box, he cheeped hours without letup. I, for one, and Pedra for another, would celebrate if he flew over the wall.

In his third week Pablito spent most days outdoors. He freely shadowed Pedra to the garden, searched for and ate ants along the sidewalk, relishing them like ball park popcorn. His scruffy appearance continued. Pin feathers thrust from his wing tips and tail. Fluffy miniature feathers blossomed through breast fuzz and he made serious efforts to preen. Although lightning fast, coordination lagged far behind his intentions and his preening attempts were ludicrous. He could not reach his breast, so with each effort fell forward like a drunken sailor. Wing-tip preening was more ridiculous, for he simply could not touch the extended stubs. He chased them in quick, tight circles until, finally dizzy, he fell in a heap. But he never stopped trying.

Compared to Pedra, his quickness was extraordinary. Darting with lightning speed around the house he chased rainbows and may have caught them for all we knew. Certainly few existed after he crossed the carpet. During devilish streaks—and they were numerous—he buzzed Pedra repeatedly. He could not pass without nuzzling under her. But before she defended, he retreated and bombed her from other azimuths with shrieks of joy on his part and groans of despair on hers.

141

For Pablito, all assaults were love-play, but for Pedra they were only hateful intrusions. I understood. Even though cornered he greased through our fingers before our fists closed. Inside his box where we owned complete advantage, he eluded us repeatedly. Pablito was fast! We always believed the speed of quail an illusion while watching families race across streets, their legs and wing stubs flapping in a beige whir. It was no illusion. Quail chicks were bred with lightning genes in their chromosomes.

Other developments proved equally interesting. At three weeks, tail feathers had grown an inch, the baby fluff nearly disappeared beneath new growth, and his voice—always persistent—noticeably lowered. Only one sound flowed from his throat, but its intensity varied. Crying, begging or threatening—he threatened anyone who would listen—Pablito achieved everything he desired with a single sound.

But he shared at least one common characteristic with his sister. Oversized feet, noticeable at hatching, remained huge. No matter how many feathers sprouted, and he owned a prodigious feather factory, his feet outdistanced all other growth. I suggested calling him Bigfoot, but Betsi hooted at the idea. Even with overlapping toes and, in danger of tripping with every step, he demonstrated remarkable agility.

Chapter Sixteen

Nimble, strong and so confidentially sure footed, Pablito flew to new frontiers. One morning he leaped experimentally but unsuccessfully to a chair. By noon he sprang to the same chair with breast-thumping success. Not content with minor victories he aimed at the couch three feet distant and fell on his head. Crash-landings never deterred him and the next morning he flew directly to a table, scratched up the cloth, sailed down to the couch as a hang glider and thence to the chair as though he had managed the same trip a thousand times. Pablito, a miracle of determination, in infancy readied himself for childhood.

If immense feet and nebulous wing stubs helped cross new rivers and foothills, razor sharp toes opened entire frontiers. Reflecting on Columbus' early voyages, Pablito too fell short of his destination. If he aimed at a tea cup in our hand, he usually missed by a quarter-inch. His toes made up the difference!

While streaking toward the cup (he seldom selected easy targets) his talons spun crazily in midair and milliseconds before landing they scratched for traction. We watched in disbelief when he finally reached the smooth tea cup lip and openly admired his aplomb, cheeping at us, eye to eye, as though the flight had been routine. He seemed unaware that only seconds ago, while whirling and scrambling toward the steaming cauldron, he had been in mortal danger of scalding to death. Somehow he never did.

Intimate flights to our shoulders, arms and neck shredded nerves, for he always landed scratching. He was not a bird to make appointments and, once he decided to visit, he moved. Leaping and clawing to our knees, he scratched his way up bare arms then, if the mood struck, jumped at our heads, leaving a trail of bleeding ears and eyebrows. Fortunately both of us wore glasses. We came to understand Pedra's impatience with her little brother, for once he arrived on our head he pecked at hair and scalp for fire ants, dandruff and lice.

We could not help but compare the two birds. Pedra flew confidently to her target. Even flights to our head proved pleasant. She nearly always achieved three-point landings and utilized her perch for an observation post. Not Pablito! He joined us in moments of frenzy, our scalps only brief resting sites for his next flight into space. His gregarious spirit and complete disregard for personal injury caused us to believe he would soon fly over the wall, for he owned an adventuresome temperament and our patio was always open. His growing independence depressed Betsi, for she saw in him great college potential, a possible Dallas Cowboy linebacker, and perhaps captain of the Olympic bobsled team.

Pablito's weight tripled in thirty days. He weighed one-and-a-half ounces and every dram was independent. Inch-long tail feathers jutted from one end and six scruffy plumes sprang from his head, giving him a distinctively unlovely appearance. But Pablito did not care if he had feathery cowlicks. Flying from chair to chair for exercise and to keep our attention, he scrambled up legs and arms, scratching a well-worn path to our head. After only a brief reconnaissance he drifted down, parachute fashion, then repeated his gymnastics. After ten minutes of assault and battery I gladly assigned Betsi full rights—with no visiting privileges—to Pablito, for he was her son. Not mine. Someplace in his innards a perpetual-motion machine balanced and I knew he intended using the afterburners until he self-destructed.

As he grew, his voice changed from a baby cheep to deeper authoritative tones and he circled the room in noisy monologues. Outside, crickets, ants and butterflies joined the endangered species for he persistently hunted and killed most moving things. A renegade's hot blood surged through his entire system. He neither loved nor respected us and no amount of yogurt, ice cream or broccoli could tempt him to us if he didn't want to visit.

"No two kids are ever the same," Betsi explained. "He'll still imprint on me. Pablito's mine!"

I hopefully agreed, but still marvelled at the differences between the two. Pedra weighed every move. She rose from her morning bed, yawned, stretched vigorously and circled two or three times—always counterclockwise—carefully looked in all directions, then confidently stepped on my waiting hand.

Pablito waited for no one. When daylight broke he invaded the world from his open applebox, hopped to the coffee table and peeped loudly, not for food, but to advertise his presence. If I offered a helping hand he flew upward, climbed over an ear and scratched my scalp.

Pedra paraded like a princess, with a careful eye across the carpet as though window shopping with money in her purse. Pablito skittered in zig-zagging flashes, always apparently on his way to an important conference. His unpredictable movements flamed with excitement, for he would streak five feet along the carpet, leap into the air squawking loudly, then turn completely about and buzz Pedra. We never knew his intentions, for neither did he. In a trip across the room he might change direction and scratch up my arm or turn 90 degrees and scare a fly on the outside of a window. Since his attention span measured between zero and a millisecond he always stayed half a step ahead of the rest of us.

Pedra never tried to outguess him, either. At least she was never ready for his unwelcome visits. If she sensed his attack, she crouched in defense as though shrinking from a hawk, all the time throating small plaintive protests. But nap time lowered her defenses. Pablito knew it and did not neglect the opportunity. Storming across the room imitating the Sioux tribe closing on General Custer at the Big Horn, he squirreled into her feathers and waved his wing stubs into her belly. With flying feathers, her dignity and nap destroyed, Pedra rose and throated multiple obscenities at him. By the time she found my receptive arm and unruffled her feathers, Pablito disappeared into the garden, challenging hummingbirds, sphinx moths and spiders.

Pedra always looked carefully before she leaped. Peering in all directions, giving special attention to ceilings, she seemed assured that God actually watched, then gracefully flew to her destination. Pablito's cluttered brain directed him to leap and, if prayer entered his thoughts, to pray. It didn't help. He banged into windows, fell from chairs and struck lampshades. We seriously considered taking portraits from patio walls for he repeatedly flew to the frames, seldom actually arriving at the frame top, but scratching across unglassed pictures. His beak, claws and fuzzy wings burst on

145

the pictures in strange, erotic designs and friends, noticing changes, asked how we achieved the special effects.

Before she flew, Pedra thoughtfully tossed her head several times in the direction of flight. We positively knew her target. Once airborne she flew directly to the destination, then carefully picked across any roadblocks and settled down, completely satisfied with an accomplished mission. Not Pablito.

Without the slightest warning he stormed from his favorite perch atop the drapes as though shot from a bow. My typewriter, in motion, presented a tempting landing field. He aimed for the action-filled platen and occasionally hit it. Failing to hit bulls-eye he careened to one side and counter-attacked the external knobs, shouting loud expletives at the machine as though it were responsible for his miss. He never jumped three inches to the platen when he failed, but preferred to dive bomb it later from the top of the drapes.

How he relished success! Striking the platen on first bounce he clung like fury and rode the carriage to its end. Although shaken by the exciting ride he was never completely unhorsed by the bucking platen. If I stopped typing briefly he scratched impatiently for action, but at the end of fifteen minutes he usually raised the flag of defeat and flew to the carpet, exhausted, as though escaping from an earthquake. Watching him cry uncle warmed my heart.

Pedra ate small grapefruit sections from a spoon. Her lady-like nibbles raised pride in us believing we had taught her proper table manners.

Pablito ate grapefruit, too, but with a difference. He sprang to the fruit without waiting for small pieces, scratching energetically into the flesh and digging for seeds. He could not possibly eat them, for he couldn't even swallow a whole sunflower seed. When faced with an entire citrus section he might vault to its center, scratch from the side or leap atop our heads. We never knew.

The most outrageous difference between them—size not counting—lay in appearance. Pedra had blossomed into a devastatingly beautiful quail. Her feathers glowed in luminescent loveliness. They begged fondling. With imagination we visualized our queen gliding down a winding staircase, immaculately groomed with a diamond tiara blazing around her plume. Pablito required no imagination. The gutsy little street urchin lived by his wits and seemed to have recently escaped from a garbage can. His tousled feathers and plume took grooming instructions from no one. Not even Pablito. An impertinent grin and formula-smeared face, never clean, even in repose, seemed poised for instant devilment. Yet we never saw him unhappy.

Pablito was not the retiring type and I sensed he would leave us at first opportunity, but Betsi knew she had discovered a son who would support her in her golden years. We were more uncertain regarding Pedra. Molting had begun and anxious males called from the wall. Observing finches playing silly games in the garden suggested mating season had arrived. Maybe we would be childless again. The depressing thought sobered us for, despite tribulations, we had come to love the quail. Even Pablito.

Chapter Seventeen

Molting was such a messy affair. A feathery snowstorm drifted around our shoes when we walked. Wing, breast and tiny fluffy feathers so small we marvelled at their perfection spread over the carpet. We picked up every one! Ultimately more than a quart of loosely packed discards nearly filled a large cut glass bowl on the bookshelf. Pablito harbored no sentiment for them. One afternoon he discovered the bowl and leaped inside. A magnificent feathery tornado erupted and, despite Betsi's thorough efforts, each of us discovered feathers in onion soup that evening. Belatedly we covered the bowl. Pedra wasted no sentiment, either. She cast feathers aside without a glance as quickly as possible and decorated the house with wispy puffs.

Pedra would quickly have been naked had she not replaced the old with new, but we could hardly believe that a bird so small could shed so many clothes. Somehow she did. They loosened and automatically dropped, drifting as she travelled. Other times she pecked them out during preening. We never had picked up as many clothes for our own children during teen age sloth.

Sometimes entire clumps fell out at once, other times, as we walked, diminutive breast feathers no larger than a buttercup petal fluttered at our feet. Betsi collected them as gold. Then, as quickly as molting started, the process stopped. A sheen we had not known blossomed and Pedra glowed in beauty. She appeared even more beautiful lying in the sun waxing her wings, eyes closed, thoroughly relaxed and napping. I had never seen a more beautiful bird. One basic molting function had been accomplished: new spring clothes. She needed them after her illnesses, but we also were aware of the second molting role: preparation for mating. Pedra was ready.

Although biased, we knew her to be the most beautiful quail in Sun City. Among thousands, in our estimation, she stood above all others. Her cheerful optimistic presence, the illnesses and recently her feathery contributions had blessed us. Most of all, her undying admiration and devotion to me remained steadfast and I hated to be cuckolded by a horny male quail.

We set strict standards for a mate and counseled Pedra regarding the sanctity of marriage, realizing her breed mated for life. We cautioned against casual affairs with balding hippies, welfare recipients and food stamp moochers, explaining that little future existed with those males. We preached God, motherhood and the American flag, concluding each lecture with the Gettysburg Address. Finally, we preferred a fast pitch softball player who paid his bills and mowed the lawn regularly on Sunday morning. Pedra listened as though she agreed and clucked quietly. In her spare time Betsi prayed a mate would be selected who needed a condominium in our backyard. Anticipating that eventuality, she furnished a love nest under the fig tree.

A blood-red sun rose that May morning when the male called from the bottle brush. Clouds fluttered in pale pink streamers across the mountains then quickly changed to startling mauve until, in an explosion of crimson, the sun leaped to the top of the white garden wall. The male quail flew confidently to the wall and, framed against the intense spotlight, called, at first, in low, seductive tones. Suddenly, his command boomed into the garden.

Pedra had dust bathed about six o'clock and her toilet completed, she pecked, scratched and shook dust among parsley and basil, completely ignoring the visitor. Her suitor fluttered for attention then paraded slowly along the wall as a colonel addressing his regiment. Leaping twice about a foot in the air, he flapped his wings loudly and this time Pedra noticed. I had never seen a more beautiful male quail. Pedra cocked an eye and raised her head, I thought, in admiration. Having captured her attention, the intruder elevated his plume, reared back, tail touching the wall, and hopped four times forward, cooing seductive invitations. Even I understood. Pedra was chosen.

Coyly Pedra seemed to lose interest and scratched more intensely into loam at her feet, then disappeared beneath a yellow snapdragon. Small delicate chirps, inconsistent with ordinary conversation, answered. I lowered *The Arizona*

Republic and stared in fascination. Our child—my bird—was leaving. I knew it!

The timing was right and, I reluctantly admitted, so was the male. Pedra had given us wonderful times and now all was finished. Betsi slept peacefully twenty feet away and I did not call her, deciding to break the news when she wakened.

The amorous lover drifted gracefully to the ground and paced through winter savory and thyme toward Pedra. Large for a Gambel's, his markings seemed extraordinarily brilliant. His red head glowed in the sunrise and, had he knocked at my garden window I would have followed him into the sunset, the moonlight or nearest motel. Finches warbled in pineapple guava branches and darted from each other in mating flurries. Love and romance filled the sky. I hardly breathed.

Suddenly his voice changed. Without let up, enticing chirps flowed from his throat and Pedra lifted her virginal head. "There's still time," I told myself. "Drive the interloper from your door! He's not good enough. No quail is good enough!" I took off my shoe to hurl though the open door.

Instinct glued me to the chair yet I urged myself, "Throw your shoe! Throw anything!" Then I watched Pedra leave the protection of the snapdragon and slowly step toward him. She balanced on the springboard of indecision, only briefly weighing possibilities of her future. Her eyes shifted rapidly, then she paused before taking the final step, burying one leg beneath her breast while listening to the powerful mating drum directly ahead. Her lover strode steadily toward her, throating insistent love sonnets.

Dry spittle plugged my mouth and prevented offering best wishes as he closed the gap. Less than two feet away she suddenly looked past him as though he did not exist, turned, never hesitating, and deliberately stepped twenty quail paces inside the patio. Moving directly to my shoe she vigorously pecked its sole. Never had she pecked harder. Solid, fierce communicative pecks told more than words. Pedra was mine and I was hers and that was that.

I shuffled the newspaper and started to read, but the newsprint blurred. Moments later print came into focus and I glanced into the garden, but the male was gone. He never returned.

Pedra snuggled inside the pocket of my arch, both eyes closed, her plume completely at rest. Her head drooped forward, nearly relaxed to the carpet and her wings folded loosely around her body. Slowly, she turned upward and cocked an eye at me. I winked back almost blowing her a kiss. She clucked softly several times in contentment, lowered her head to the floor, and slept at my toes.

Pedra was mine now. When Pablito left, his good-byes could not be so traumatic...at least to my way of thinking.

Chapter Eighteen

Several phobias, possibly based on gypsy warnings, struck terror into Pedra's fluttering heart. She never outgrew her fear of unexpected shadows. Any overhead silhouette plunged her into a passion of horror. Once they had been sighted, she blinked, crouched and froze as though in bronze. Then, as a lightning flash, she scurried to the nearest cover even though it was only a twig and hopelessly inadequate. Again she struck point praying for invisibility, preferring an armored bunker or bank vault to a scanty marigold bush. Our beautiful bird crouched quietly long after the shadow disappeared, then carefully cocked an eye skyward and reassured herself with small comforting coos that she had survived another potential disaster. Only then did Pedra fluff feathers, clean her beak in nervous swipes, and stalk carefully from concealment.

The briefest shadow ruffled her feathers beyond belief. While dust bathing in the herb patch a single humming bird flew above, she dove instantly into thyme foliage and froze. More than once during winter months when sunlight flooded the patio and Pedra luxuriated on the carpet, a shadowy cloud of finches fluttered by. Springing from security behind glassed walls, she fled squeaking to protective chairs, tables or my arm.

Pedra also considered brooms the devil's tool and avoided them as a plague. She could not tolerate their sight. If one appeared in the kitchen, she flew to the refrigerator top, chattering loudly, her head darting about, fearful of the broom's destructive path. Her loud protests encouraged us— and the broom—to leave. She could sense the kitchen needed sweeping and before the dangerous interloper came in sight, quick circling steps indicated she knew about our mission of terror and disclosed she did not approve. Before the broom actually appeared, Pedra disappeared, sometimes as far away as the bed or bathroom. For her, twentieth century tidiness could have survived without brooms.

She classified vacuum cleaners as noisy brooms and the sight of the upright cleaner with cord and attachment spoiled her day. Only her loud caterwauling protests overpowered its sound. Not easily intimidated by many things, the vacuum set her on fire. At its appearance she, if possible, would have placed wings over her ears, closed her eyes and conjured it out of this world. She did the next best thing, leaving the room in a flutter and hiding beneath the bed, crying for peace and abolition of all vacuum cleaners.

Once a friend loaned us a metal detector. Pedra tagged it an unwelcome cousin of the hated vacuum and with sharp protests, vanished. When her tail disappeared into the bedroom, she glanced backward as though she planned an exceedingly long memory regarding metal detectors.

Whistles would set her gizzard whirring. Any whistle, even a teakettle. We suspected whistling might be a witch's signal not known to us. Otherwise why the violent reaction?

Betsi and I whistle. We're born whistlers. We whistle in astonishment, for joy, despair or to attract attention. While working, both concentrating, our low, almost imperceptible whistles signal gentle attention between us. Neither demanding nor alarming, it is our special cue. We quickly reestablish lost contact in large department stores with low, penetrating whistles. In woods and mountains, for many happy years, we communicated by whistling. It was our second language. Friends were surprised when told about our whistling communication claiming never having heard us, although we signaled a thousand times in their presence. Pedra was more observant.

Sharp whistles of astonishment sent her wings flying. Low appreciative ones raised neck feathers and she stalked back and forth issuing warning signals. Additional low— barely audible—whistles brought forth noisy wing flutters and her rapid head-bobbing was a certain sign of disapproval. A third whistle, if we were that unobservant, caused complete disappearance for she did not issue idle threats. So a lifelong habit disappeared when Pedra came to us. We stopped whistling.

How did she know fly swatters familied with brooms and vacuums? Somehow she did. She faced the disasters of pneumonia, spider venom and yolk peritonitis without complaint, yet a fly swatter's appearance suggested death

154

and our bird turned to jelly. Her phobia proved fortunate since she developed an over-curious attitude regarding visitor's jewelry. Let dangling earrings appear and Pedra instantly flew to the ear, rapping bold investigative pecks on the metal and diamonds. After repeated choruses in their ears, many female friends suddenly recalled pressing and forgotten meetings. Their quick departures sometimes annoyed us, but quieted the air, for conversation was difficult when, apparently, a team of woodpeckers had invaded, the room.

Bracelets, diamond watches and barrettes all sounded a call to colors and Pedra never failed to answer the challenge. Equally irritating was her foot-and-shoe fetish. She communicated with vigorous pecks at most shoes, especially the soles. Bare feet and sandals caused most problems for, after pecking around toenails and discovering lint, sand and interesting trace elements, she probed the possibilities of the ankle bone, sometimes surrounding it with a series of sharp nips. Not even the most courteous friend sat unmoved under Pedra's attention, so we sometimes banished her to the bedroom or garden.

We asked the molestees to punt her into the next room, but they never did. It seemed ill-mannered to kick at a seven-ounce feathery fluff who sprang away, observing their futile efforts from a safe distance, for kicking Pedra and kicking AT her were two different things. Pedra survived! She had not lived with us nearly a year without learning about strange men and women who talked of cancer, bladder inflammation and great grandchildren. Betsi finally suggested a solution.

When dangling earrings flashed through the yard or a red pair of sneakers approached from the garden, Pedra waited inside as though tugging at a leash. On entrance we handed the guest a fly swatter. Pedra's Jekyll-Hyde personality altered instantly and she wilted into a whimpering marshmallow. Instead of imitating a bloodthirsty Doberman, she shrank out of sight, watching as guests with fascinating earrings and tempting rubber-soled shoes enjoyed a Pedra-free environment.

No one ever struck her with the swatter, yet she feared it as the rack and never approached a person so armed. Having learned its advantages, we hung the swatter on a cup hook near the kitchen table. If Pedra overstepped her privileges we reached for the swatter and she vanished in a second with a series of wild, staccato yelps. Then, with time on her hands and the swatter hanging innocently on the cup hook, she inspected the hanging weapon, walking in slow circular motions around it, chirping low curses.

Although we never jested publicly about Pedra's phobias we were privately amused. Under no circumstances had she been injured by shadows or brooms or conditioned by us to fear them. Instinct greater than reason overpowered her and we could not understand.

Late one spring evening Betsi and I listened to evening news and waited for pot stew and cornbread. Fresh tea steamed and cold onion-orange salad marinated in the refrigerator. Cannas and bougainvillea washed the wall with irregular red splashes while a chorus of finches chattered, for they claimed championship as the greatest gossips in the garden. A pair of Inca doves listened intently, unable to compete with the accomplished tattlers. Suddenly all sound vanished as though sucked into a vacuum and the gentle autumn breeze trembled momentarily, then died.

Betsi suddenly gasped, clasped her mouth and pointed to the wall. "Look!" she cried. A fleeting shadow followed by a towering Cooper's hawk calmly glided to the white wall scarcely thirty feet away. His piercing beak, ominously sharp in silhouette, twisted gradually and he strolled to the wall's corner. Not a whisper surfaced in the garden. "Where are the kids?" Betsi whispered as though in a library, then she grasped my wrist tightly and growled through the window, "Go away hawk!"

Both quail prowled during twilight combining pre-dinner play with dust bathing. They enjoyed complete outdoor freedom and we did not monitor them closely. Small gray foxes and an occasional coyote penetrated condominium defenses, but we had seen none and did not worry. Many hawks hunted along fences and power lines when we drove desert roads, and we watched their gliding and hunting tactics far above us, but we had never seen them in our garden. Hawks were expert hunters. Mice, varmints and snakes—even quail—provided food. It was not a comforting thought, for the Cooper's hawk strolling on our wall appeared exceedingly famished.

The hawk pivoted and retraced its route staring intently downward. No sign of life existed. Not a leaf dropped and shadows froze as absolute silence reigned. "Thank God the finches saw him in time," I said. "There's not a bird in the garden."

Betsi did not agree. "Finches are there. So are Pedra and Pablito."

"No, they're gone," I argued. "Our quail are someplace in the house."

"Pedra and Pablito are outside," Betsi insisted. Her eyes, large as zinnias, never left the hawk.

The plunderer eyed the foliage and spread its wings parachute fashion above us. Although only a three-foot wing span, it seemed to cover the entire garden as he bobbed quietly to the rosemary plant ten feet away. Even behind double-thick thermopane he intimidated us more than any bird we had ever faced and we had nursed both golden and bald eagles in earlier times. He strode confidently along the gravel glaring into basil, thyme and savory, but when he reached the sidewalk directly in front of us our hypnotic trance snapped. Betsi grasped the broom and sped to the patio in long strides, shouting insults. Leisurely, the predator airlifted over the fence and lofted high in the dusky desert. A moment later he was an insignificant speck.

"Let's find the kids," Betsi said and hurried to the garden.

I smiled. "There's nothing here. Couldn't be. Everything flew soon as the hawk approached. Birds have a sixth sense about those things," I patiently told her. "Nothing's here."

Betsi plunged the broom into geraniums, phlox and tomato plants with decisive strokes and finches exploded like firecrackers on New Year's eve. From under her feet as though a magician had waved his wand, dozen of birds scrambled away. In another second more than fifty sparrows, finches and a confused mockingbird flushed from cover and disappeared over the wall.

I stared in awe. "That's survival," I muttered. "Let's go inside and find the kids."

Before reaching the sidewalk a low chirp erupted from an oversized basil plant. Pedra's beak pressed from the foliage and she stared at us with cautious eyes. Pablito was not in sight. Then Pedra found her voice and sharp staccato commands scolded us but she remained under the herb's protective leaves. No amount of coaxing teased her to us and she continued ranting.

"She blames us for the hawk," I said.

"She blames me for the broom," Betsi replied and flung the culprit, end over end, at the garage door.

Only then did Pedra's head emerge, her dark gray body close to the earth as though half buried. Tentatively she crept, step by step, from the basil. Then we saw Pablito in a tight shadow, huddled protectively under his sister and moving in one motion with her. Pedra tipped her head skyward, glared disdainfully at the sky and at the discarded broom, then marched into the patio and cleaned her beak noisily on the carpet. Pablito followed.

Happiness swept over us when we slid the door closed, but Pedra's tense face and vigorous scratching did not echo our sense of relief. She started barking, almost dog-like, at us. An unrepentant cacophony burst from her vibrating throat. She balanced on her toes, her extended neck pointed like an index finger to the garden. Her head bobbed excitedly and, incoherent with repressed fear, she could not be quieted. After a minute or two, her spring ran down and she leaped to the table, pecked viciously at broccoli, while sporadically glancing through the window.

Pablito had forgotten the hawk and calmly preened new feathers under his lamp, all danger miraculously forgotten. Pedra still pecked in frustration at the table top, spitting expletives at us and searching around for brooms, shadows and hawks, all the time keeping a constant eye on the hanging fly swatter.

"We'll never laugh about Pedra's phobias again," Betsi reminded me.

And we didn't. Shadows or brooms, Pedra knew best.

Chapter Nineteen

Beginning the third week of life, Pablito, runt of the flock, was about as happy as a quail can be. He could scratch his ear standing on one foot, eat ten meals daily, and continue his love affair with Pedra. Baby-down barely dotted his face and distinctive brown stripes streaked across his head with light beige borders. Dark-throated male markings and a ruddy topknot added a dashing flair to his perpetual grin. Appearing as a masked clown, he could easily have been mistaken for a highwayman, too. His birth weight remained constant despite an enlarged diet, for he expended tremendous energy exploring his limited world. But he survived and gained strength, if not ounces, every day.

Spiny pin feathers springing from wing tips in quiet spurts greatly enlarged his world. With athletic legs and half-inch feathers he quickly leaped into space (only a foot at a time, it's true) discovering new worlds and thrilling with each revelation.

Fearless was his name. Loud noises, height and big sister did not intimidate him. Neither did death, for that matter. He never gave it a second thought. Cocking an ear skyward during sonic booms he continued calmly cheeping to himself, considering his personal conversation the best advice. He certainly listened to no other.

If Pablito missed his bearings during flight and plunged downward in a nosedive, somehow he landed running, always in a hurry. Happiness with life surmounted all obstacles and, if big sister pecked him, he quickly dodged the second peck and buried beneath her breast, wiggling and nudging in a most unbrotherly fashion. Adversity, it seemed, toughened and sharpened his survival wits.

His general untidiness concerned Betsi greatly. Pedra had been such a beautiful baby before her deforming plunge to the floor. Pablito was a mess. Matted down remained glued around him in untidy patterns, pin feathers erupted at divergent angles with small hope of assuming an orderly arrangement, and the plume, pride of all Gambel's, curved into a corkscrew. He tackled food like a tiger and he dumped it into his craw in loud smacking bites, smearing seeds, chaff and dirt along with any nutritious food that might have mistakenly been consumed. Cleaning his beak, he instinctively wiped dirt and muck along his mouth so, like eating mudpies, his mouth seldom was clean as he flew to us grinning and chirping with a face always covered with formula jam.

Despite his ungainly appearance, Pablito owned the quickest reflexes on the block. Minuscule downy breast feathers further streamlined him and oversized legs and feet supplemented his speed. He scheduled random flights with the confidence of a paratrooper, erratically but confident. Capturing him without a butterfly net resembled chasing shadows in a windstorm. Even when cornered, with our hands closing around Pablito, he sometimes disappeared so rapidly we did not feel him slip though our fingers. Small wonder he caught flies in midair.

Pablito ran from the house as freely as Pedra and quickly discovered the herb patch. He staked bathing rights in shade of the aromatic English thyme bush and mimicked Pedra, for they shared the same area. Quickly pecking a hole, he enthusiastically entered a dust bathing world. Pedra contented herself with a bath or two daily. Pablito cleaned a dozen times or more, at times like a child repeatedly sliding down a playground chute. He did not bathe intensively, for his minimal attention span refused that luxury, but did perform cameo bathing exercises throughout the day. We gave him several standing ovations.

Whereas Pedra emerged from her bath tired and shiny, Pablito sprang from his hole exhilarated and messy, ready for another dip. We positively marvelled at his talent for appearing dirtier after bathing than before. I despaired of teaching him cleanliness, but Betsi persisted.

The three composed an extraordinary trio. Ounce-and-a-half Pablito, resembling a runaway short-bed truck, raced in and out of training sessions, snatching bits of food and lesser amounts of information. Pedra, regal and intelligent, perched calmly at the broccoli jig giving complete attention to Betsi. Betsi, the bird-like Aristotle, loved both birds passionately, constantly rapped her plastic sunflower seed box for attention. From a distance the trio sounded like off-key calliopes.

But one day Pedra's serene world exploded. We noticed the change overnight. Instead of an extroverted loving nature, a sulky and devious personality emerged. Refusing our company she marched continuously across the carpet challenging us with sharp, unhappy cries, then erratically hurrying to us as though she had forgotten something. Attempted dust baths left her dissatisfied and she returned inside the house unbathed and crying.

"She's jealous," Betsi said. "She doesn't like Pablito."

I did not argue, for Pedra never had gracefully accepted her young, hell-raising brother and, for that matter, neither had I.

The dilemma raised problems never anticipated and prayer for a peek inside her tiny cranium never materialized. She kept us in the dark regarding the source of her unhappiness.

Worse yet, she initiated frightening splashes against patio windows so dramatic and thundering we feared serious injury, the least of which might be a broken pane. Her sense of direction, never good, vanished and we worried about brain damage or another broken neck from her daily frontal assaults. She flew to the ceiling fan, mercifully off, and perched at the blade's edge staring down at us like a mad scarecrow. Sudden noisy flights carried her to picture frames, canting them crazily across the wall in an astigmatic arrangement. We both developed headaches, Betsi suffered a painfully stiff neck, and our heads cocked semi-permanently askew mentally readjusting the damage. Then Pedra tackled lamps shades and hung inside, bat-like, all the time uttering soft, plaintive wails. We suffered nearly as much as she but Pablito gained another ounce.

One afternoon my quail simply disappeared. I called an hour without success. Pedra always answered me, but now elected to remain quiet. We thought she had left us, but Betsi discovered her early that evening perched on the highest living room bookshelf hidden between *Saints and Sinners* and *The Discovery and Conquest of Mexico*. Breathing heavily and refusing Betsi's help, she flew to the Mongolian firepot, clutched its lip and, balancing precariously for three hours, wailed continually.

161

The next afternoon we discovered her in the garage washroom, wormed inside a pigeonhole containing aluminum foil, plastic wrap and waxed paper boxes. Working ten minutes, with no help from Pedra, we finally extricated her from her cave. Our gregarious and loving Pedra had become a hermit!

Pedra also stopped reading *The Arizona Republic* with me. I held her on my lap while she sobbed mournful messages, disdaining the editorial pages and even favorites comic strips. Betsi held tempting broccoli under her beak, but she refused it. Most disturbing, Pedra ceased napping with me. She had slept, uninvited, on my chest the past four months. Her soft feathers under my nose, while she cooed and clucked, settled my nerves and I did not rest comfortably without them tickling my throat. Now, moping under the bed or atop crooked picture frames, she disdained even me.

Perhaps worst of all, she generated behavioral changes in both of us. We, too, moped about the house, growling at each other and blaming sleepless nights on humidity, or lack of it and on the Russians. After an especially restless night Betsi bumped into the bathroom door, her fingers shot to a rapidly rising knot on her forehead and she clutched madly for support on the wall. Instead she staggered into the clutch of family portraits hanging guard there and managed to tilt the entire row into a state of drunkenness including Aunt Sarah, who never had touched a drop.

After swearing loudly Betsi cried, "I sure don't know what's wrong with Pedra, but it's something erythrocmycin or vitamins won't cure. Let's call our bird specialist." She hurried to the telephone and called the veterinarian who unfortunately vacationed in the Bahamas and would not return for a month.

Before we could call other sources Pedra climbed aboard my wrist, seized loose skin and squatted. She never had pecked me, but now her beak nearly pierced through the epidermis. I almost heard her grunt. Instead, still pinching she leaned backward and vibrated. Eyes closed, she tightened her grip on me and her entire body shuddered.

"She's laying an egg!" Betsi cried. Of course! Why hadn't we considered that possibility? Her timing was perfect. All quail except Pedra were mating and she hadn't given us an egg for five months. How could we have been so stupid? But no egg appeared.

The thought occurred to me that Pedra might enjoy a sort of tonic following her traumatic experience and I prepared a double Scotch whisky for her. She disdained the medicine and disappeared, whimpering, into the bathroom where she climbed atop the shower head and hung nearly upside down. Rather than discard the drink (I pride myself on stirring an excellent Scotch), I drank it in three gulps. Generosity overcame me and I mixed another, this time for Betsi who did not drink. When Betsi's Scotch evaporated I realized it was time to take care of my own thirst and poured another double. A comforting coziness stole over me and Pedra's wails faded as though filtered through baffled walls. When Betsi returned, far too late, she appeared to be climbing through a concave crazy-house mirror.

I found an egg next day at ten o'clock in my bathroom. The brown and beige spattered jewel rested in my shoe and measured almost twice the size of any previous egg. Its appearance did not solve her problem—or ours—for she continued crying non-stop. Attempted flights though air conditioning grills near the ceiling agonized us, but she sailed again and again toward the sealed duct, seizing metal with her beak and toes trying to gain entrance through closed aluminum. Her desperate itch for a nesting place resulted in a great hide-and-seek game as she laid secret eggs, about one a day, throughout the house.

Betsi accepted Pedra's challenge head-on. Within minutes of the first egg's discovery Betsi pronounced herself a nest builder and fashioned bird homes in both bathrooms. Pedra ignored the cotton-filled, Hilton-style bins, so Betsi modified the nest plan and built natural homes of leaves and twigs, even calling a discarded finch nest into action. Pedra did not notice. Betsi placed the finch nest atop the refrigerator for Pedra's approval, but she shunned it as a leper colony. Daily cries and moans filled the house until noon, then the young mother-to-be disappeared and eventually rejoined us, relieved. She had hidden another egg.

When Sherlock Betsi shadowed, Pedra did not lay. If Betsi waited until noon, Pedra laid an egg at eleven o'clock, for she had developed a hidden cunning we never expected and, diabolically, exploited it to the fullest. Not once was Betsi successful and it did not amuse her. She despises defeat.

On the fourth day Betsi cancelled all commitments and searched nonstop in frantic efforts to outwit the little quail.

All failed. Yet Pedra provided plenty of clues, leading Betsi to the threshold of discovery, then thwarting her at the last moment. Betsi even stopped watching her favorite soapie, for an egg had appeared directly under her nose and the next crisis could develop any time.

Pedra mounted small safaris into the garden as though she were saddled with a three-pack-a-day habit and suddenly had lost her last smoke. She fled among staked tomatoes, closely followed by a sniffing Betsi who used classic investigating procedures, even contemplating a deer hunter's cap and hand lens. Pedra scratched diversionary nests under spreading pfitzers as Betsi squinted though binoculars. When Pedra wandered into the herb patch, Betsi cultivated an intense interest in thyme, savory and marjoram but discovered only false leads. And so our personal soap opera continued, Pedra crying with morning sickness and Betsi wailing in frustration.

A sense of quiet relief overcame me the morning Betsi said she had heard an ominous scratching on our bedroom ceiling during the night and undiscovered quail eggs temporarily slid to number two priority in our disrupted lives. A Queen's Anne palm occupied the bedroom corner outside and comforted us with gentle swishes against the window. "It's the palm tree brushing against the window," I said.

"It isn't a palm tree," Betsi said as though I had stepped on a painful corn. "I know the difference between an animal and a palm tree. There's an animal up in our attic." She stabbed at the ceiling above the bed with a positive thumb.

"You've been looking for too many eggs," I said, thankful that at least Pablito and I retained a degree of sanity although this was doubtful at times. But the next night I too heard a noise resembling a badger digging through sandstone. The unpleasant scratching originated directly over my pillow and it was no palm tree. We listened carefully and Pedra, who observed the strange noise too, flew from bed and cocked her head anxiously skyward.

"I'll stop the racket," I told Betsi. "Put Pedra in bed while I find a broom." Three stout thumps on the ceiling and the disruption vanished. Pedra cried a few minutes, but Pablito slept through the entire crisis.

The next morning Betsi pointed at the ceiling. "Look what your palm tree did." Plaster, sawdust and insulation covered the bed and a quarter-sized hole opened into the attic. Uninvited guests were coming to share bed and breakfast. They didn't seem the sort we would loan our Skil saw or lawnmower to, even for an hour.

The exterminator representative arrived promptly. During the telephone conversation Betsi indicated the house was in immediate danger of disappearing and the man's truck skidded near the gate. The exterminator had visions of seeing only sawdust inside the wall. He was fat and wore a white jacket. A company emblem blazed in neon red above his breast pocket. The symbol gave him an authority that I had doubted on first glance, but he waddled breathlessly through the patio, into the bedroom and squinted up. His mouth fell ajar. "Lady," he said scratching his head, "I ain't never seen nuthin' like that before."

"I ain't neither," Betsi replied. "What can you do?"

The man examined his fingernails for foreign matter and retrieved a penknife from his pocket, proceeding to clean dandruff and debris with deliberate surgical skill. Finally he said, "If they was bugs, I could spray but they ain't. Ain't no bug never made holes like them and I can't spray something I don't know what they is." Then folding the small blade he returned the knife to his pocket.

"I think it's a cotton rat," Betsi ventured.

Pedra and Pablito had accompanied the man into the bedroom and flew to the bed, examining his belly pushing though the bottom two shirt buttons. The man stared at the quail, but did not believe his eyes. Both birds returned his glance, Pedra scrutinizing him as if trying to relate him to a wanted poster in a post office lobby.

"Lady, whatthehell is them?" he asked, pointing a stubby finger at Pedra. Pablito, in the middle of a St. Vitus dance, defied anyone to track him.

"They're our friends," Betsi explained. "They live with us."

The man's knees buckled under the unexpected information and might have completely given way, but he grasped his stomach with both hands and tugged upward. Amazement raced across his face and instinct warned him against further questions. Waddling in a random manner, he found the garden and, outside, breathed deeply.

"What do you think is up there?" Betsi asked. The man stared as if he had seen her for the first time then shook his head. "What's in the attic?" she persisted. "Are they cotton rats, ostriches or elephants?"

"Not ostriches," he told her, then seemed to regain awareness, jabbing short fingers toward the bedroom. "Yeah, rats. That's it. Rats." Glancing at his stomach he added, "I can't get up in no attic, so you better get some rat poison up there damn quick or you ain't gonna have no ceiling."

"We'll do it," she told him. "We like our ceiling, thank you. How much do we owe for your help?"

"Owe? Owe?" The man seemed confused as if it were a Greek word. "Nothin'. I don't charge nothin' for nothin'." And mumbling more to himself than to the quail following him, he continued, "I ain't never seen no rat hole in no ceiling and no quail in no bed, neither!"

An hour later his wife called. "Jed says you folks have quail in your bed and they sleep with you. Is that true?" Betsi admitted at least part of the accusation was correct. His wife continued. "How many are there?" and Betsi admitted we owned two. "I wondered about that," his wife said. "Jed's been seeing double lately."

Betsi crawled into the attic armed with rat poison within an hour and two nights later all activity ceased. We never discovered the identity of our Peeping Tom neighbor. "He never met us either." Betsi told friends, "So it all worked out for the best."

It certainly did. In the garage on her way from the attic she tipped the cover of a clay pot cooker and revealed Pedra's secret. Seven beige and brown eggs lay inside.

The mystery discovered, that noon Pedra returned to my chest for her daily nap, her first in over a week. Her petticoat feathers dropped, and she strained near my chin. It was no easy strain trembling and squatting over my chest. With fluffed feathers her body seemed twice normal size. Her tail vibrated against my throat as she went into labor. Delivery was strenuous. For three excruciating minutes she cried and pressed against my chin. Suddenly a warm moist egg dropped in the hollow of my throat, its shell popping faintly as it hardened. Pedra rose, shook feathers and faced me mentally and physically exhausted. She had delivered her ultimate gift.

Each delivery became less traumatic and during the next six weeks Pedra laid thirty-two eggs. Forty-one alto-

166

gether and always on my chest or throat with two exceptions. One noon I did not arrive home and she hopped up to Betsi and dropped an egg in her hand. The second time she inexplicably went to Betsi during my nap and deposited an egg on Betsi's lap as sort of a consolation prize. We labeled each sterile gift according to time and date and encased them in one of Pedra's rejected nests.➤

Chapter Twenty

After forty-one deliveries, Pedra's anxieties ceased. Egg production quit, too, and we set her collection under the glass-lined coffee table as in a museum cabinet. She no longer flew into patio windows, picture frames or lampshades and we erased scratch marks from heat vents along the ceiling. Her continuous, persistent, piercing cries modulated into pleasant chatter and she leaped on *The Arizona Republic* each morning and, together we scanned editorial pages, sports coverage and Peanuts. So a normalcy of sorts prevailed when Pedra's appetite, and ours, returned.

Both quail ate nearly everything. In addition to basic formula Betsi plumped their diets with vitamins and fresh produce. They also pillaged the garden for craw-sand and protein supplements...ants, flies and young crickets. Neither objected to culinary experimentation and sometimes tackled exotic food with strange results.

Anchovies was one. Both birds leaped to the kitchen counter one pleasant evening as I prepared salad and observed with more than ordinary interest when I pried open a tin of anchovies. Their perpetual curiosity increased and they moved closer. Pedra waited with itching toes until the stripped tin opened and then she plunged full force into the salty hors d'oeuvre. The impact of the fishy fumes staggered her and she limped backward, looking at me as a betrayed woman. She would have gagged if possible, but lacking that talent, shook her head as if to shout, "No! No!", and clacked her beak on a towel to cleanse her mouth, glancing at me occasionally to hear my apologies. Her eyes seldom strayed from the open tin, staring as though a black cat had crossed her path or she had spotted an upturned ace of spades at a gypsy's table.

Pablito shadowed his sister and, far from accepting her decision, wolfed down an anchovy in three great chomps. Not hesitating after the first bite, he madly and instantly converted to anchovies, and stepped into the oily can with both feet, claiming sole rights to its contents. Anchovies remained a favorite forever. Even though he did not tell us how much he enjoyed the small, oily fish we knew for he attacked all flat tins resembling anchovy containers no matter the shape (he read labels indifferently) and one morning nearly scratched all paint from a closed can of shoe polish.

Both birds enjoyed whipped cream and creamed cheese at first peck and would have sold their feathery souls for ice cream. Pecking into a teaspoon filled with frozen dessert they never stopped until headaches halted gluttony. Fascinated, we watched our birds plough into teaspoons of fresh ice cream—they would not eat it once melted—then peck deep furrows through the frozen custard, heads nearly disappearing as if in quicksand. Suddenly they stopped and backed from the spoon, violently shaking their heads trying to stop temporal headaches. Again and again they struggled to eliminate the ache, staring with open eyes in mute pleas for relief. Yet moments later, when pain subsided, they returned and slurped until their craws filled because, for them, ice cream was a wonder. We understood.

Fresh and dried fruit climbed the quail culinary ladder together. They stole Bing cherries from bowls and scurried away, quickly consuming everything but skin and pits. They fervently sought dates, raspberries, pineapple guavas and seasonal papaya, ravishing it on sight. If we ate, they ate, although sometimes quite differently.

Popcorn intoxicated their souls and they fluttered to the counter at the air popper's appearance, plunging into the stimulating world of fresh, buttered popcorn. Circling the exploding kernels like hungry rats, they waited eagerly as popcorn bombs detonated and if a kernel escaped, they dashed madly after it. They never mastered the trick of securing the popped corn into corners or anchoring it with their feet but chased popcorn like loose ping pong balls across the floor. So Betsi hand-fed them. Sometimes she teased Pablito by withholding the delicacy an inch from his beak and under such circumstances he acted as though he had been kicked in the groin. Regaining his breath, he shouted insults at Betsi for he was not a bird of tremendous restraint. Once the treat was reduced to chaff he waited expectantly for another and when his craw filled, enthusiasm for popcorn vanished and he staggered to a quiet corner and slept for an hour.

Neither could swallow large black watermelon seeds, but welcomed every white, immature one tossed their direction. When we sectioned a fresh melon, both quail waited impatiently on the sidelines as we pinched white slippery seeds at them. Sometimes the seeds sailed high into the air and, discovering the flight pattern, both flew as fighter planes toward a common enemy. If they arrived simultaneously, sometimes a squabble over ownership developed before one ate it. Then they returned to the home base watermelon and waited for the next mission. Their wait usually was short, for we were as anxious to continue the game as they.

If, when we pinched the seed and it fell as a dud in front of them, they mentally flipped a coin to determine who would field the cripple. Neither favored an easy score, for they loved the spirit of the chase above all else. Plainly they enjoyed games and so did we. Watermelon feasts pleasured all of us including myself who had never fancied watermelon before.

One morning Betsi brought fresh strawberries from the market and rolled a berry in their direction. After a spirited chase around the kitchen table, they finally anchored it with a foot apiece and ate, not the flesh, but all of the nearly invisible seeds scattered around its surface. Kiwi slices received identical treatment. They ate all seeds, leaving delectable flesh for us, and rambled through cucumber slices like watermelon, nearly burying their heads in frantic dives for fresh treasure.

When their craws filled, our birds played other games, worrying prune and date pits across the carpet and under the refrigerator. We discovered dessicated fruit remains in strange places while walking barefooted and the vacuum rattled dreadful warnings at us when date pits lay hiding. Grapefruit, apple and cantaloupe seeds all provided play toys and the quail gamboled, alone and in pairs, tossing and pushing the rejects around the floor.

How they loved bones! The first time Pedra tackled a chicken leg we accused her of cannibalism, but she did not listen, for instinctively she loved all bones, especially joints. After we cleaned the flesh from a chicken thigh, she continued pecking, prying and shoving the discarded bone over the table in messy patterns. We saw neither food nor promise in the cooked bone, but Pedra relished the morsel beyond imagination. So did Pablito. Once he discovered the treasure inside, he plunged vigorously into spare ribs and T-bone steak carcasses. He seemed to enjoy barbecue ribs most of all because they were messier. Watching the pair tumbling about a cleaned chicken leg we decided the necessity for a garbage disposal or compactor had virtually disappeared.

Their culinary interest heated to such a rapid boil that sometimes we wondered what their next whim might be, especially when they discovered garlic and chives. But then, love of garlic was no whim for Gambel's quail. Both posted five-star blessings on the stinking lily family and they devoured it at every opportunity. We did not encourage garlic breakfasts, for they could have eaten so many other less objectionable foods early in the day. But that was not their way.

A hanging string of braided garlic above the refrigerator tempted Pedra beyond belief. She not only enjoyed the warm draft-free area, but garlic aroma stimulated her senses and she devoted many aromatic hours there. Within days she easily devoured the nearest cloves, then performed acrobatic antics to obtain those slightly out of reach. With her toes firmly embedded in a towel on the refrigerator she stretched her neck, crane-like, downward and coaxed the garlic closer. It swung and she nibbled. Within a month she devoured three pounds of high quality Greek garlic and we could smell her from the bedroom. She relished it so much we allowed its total destruction, but did not replace the vanished, expensive hors d'oeuvre. A memento of her determination—and love of garlic—remained, for Pedra left the outside skins intact. They appeared nearly unblemished. Only the papery shell remained as a decoration.

Chinese chives produced equally strong results. The herb grew like weeds most of the year and we used them generously. So did quail! Pedra and Pablito quickly developed an affinity for the tender shoots, but couldn't cope easily with tougher mature stems. Betsi spoiled them. She patiently sectioned stems lengthwise into long thin strings and the birds slurped them like spaghetti. A six-inch piece slipped down their throats in three seconds flat, in a single continuous, peristaltic swallow.

Fascinated visitors watched while the quail impatiently waited their turn. Chive-eating was one of their best acts. But how their breath stank! We could barely tolerate them after a chive banquet, and that's when they leaped to our shoulders with exciting information to tell us. Although Chinese chives ranked as one of the delicate onion family members, we did not believe authorities. Apparently they never had smelled two stinking quail following a chive meal. For us, chive potency surpassed garlic—maybe we tolerated garlic more—and seldom fed them chive strips except at bedtime. Most odor dissipated, from both digestive directions, during the night.

Our bird family viewed onions through rose-colored glasses and, indeed, we classified onion breath less offensive than garlic or chives. Yet both birds enjoyed onions just as much. The first sign of onion, green or dry, loosened a spring in their craw and they fluttered as a team to the chopping board, pecking small bites near the cutting blade. We wondered why they did not lose toes or entire feet as they incautiously veered under the knife. Both birds allowed us to worry about amputation, and we did, for Pablito at times dared us to decapitate him. How could we know, though we would later discover, he saved his neck for other escapades?

Pedra, especially, cooed heavenly songs during garlic harvest. Our small garden produced bountiful supplies of elephant garlic, for we planted it in every available cranny. Harvesting in June, Pedra immediately offered her services as taster when garlic appeared on the cutting block. She had not been allowed in the den during the drying period for reasons of gluttony, but now leaped to the kitchen table expectantly. Four pounds of prime garlic lay within reach and she hardly knew where to begin. We did.

Food processed garlic, sealed in oil and refrigerated, lasted a year. We had prepared it many years without Pedra's help, but she insisted on doing so now. In her eagerness, she hopped to the bowl's lip and slipped at once into a quart of oiled garlic! Far from an accident, it appeared part of her plan. Her feet traced a booming dance in the bowl as though stomping grapes and she quickly saturated all her feathers while gulping great swallows of oil and garlic.

She peered up at me happier than in months. Her chin, dripping in garlic-oil, was not Pedra's at all, but the ghost of Pablito grinning in triumph. Maybe they enjoyed closer filial relations than we suspected. For an instant I found myself thoroughly enjoying the garlic swim almost as much as she, but common sense surfaced and deodorizing problems faced me. All attempts proved equally ineffective. Detergents, perfume and even skunk-scent removing tomato juice failed, and for weeks friends sniffed suspiciously, but did not comment, when Pedra leaped to their laps. Even Pablito gave her a wide berth. Had we believed in reincarnation we might have thought Pedra's ancestors flew from the Greek islands or even Italy.

Although nothing could be further removed from vegetables, dried bread crumbs and uncooked cream of wheat also rated high on both bird's grocery lists. And of course our educated quail ate from a spoon. If we spread food on the table they ignored it, but once it was inside a spoon they tapped small, exciting melodies until every crumb vanished. We always enjoyed the duet.

Pablito's water dish tendered a musical solo quite different from cream of wheat or bread crumbs. This discovery came about accidentally. We had searched unsuccessfully for a suitable water dish to place on the carpet. Every dish had been quickly overturned and the area suggested a swamp. We watered the quail on the table as well as the carpet, but for unknown reasons they only ruined the carpet watering hole.

Betsi suggested the solution. Digging into a closet corner known mainly to earwigs and black scaly beetles, she retrieved an ancient brass, futuristic cornucopia dull with oxidation. It had been given to us by persons whose home was decorated in deep purple and mauve. The ugly monstrosity white-elephanted about the house, burrowing deeper into shelves and boxes until we no longer displayed it even when the donors visited.

Finally we found a suitable use since the hideous eyesore offered a perfect drinking dish for the birds. They could not overturn the heavy brass horn but easily drank from its shallow draft. Additionally, the warty lip offered an ideal bar rail for Pablito's feet.

He scratched from the day he joined us and gathered enough strength to move. We diagnosed it as protest. When he grew, he compulsively scratched all sand and dirt, our hands and arms, the bare kitchen counter and one time leaped into the middle of a startled guest's quiche and flung custard toward four walls and a sizable blob in her left eye.

174

We especially enjoyed his drinking habits. His routine never varied. Approaching the water dish he scratched several inches from the receptacle and by the time he reached target his feet fairly flew. It was the overwhelming reason the rug resembled the Okefenokee Swamp. After digging into carpet like a chainsaw his engine slowed and he drank long satisfying drafts, one foot perched on the rim. He never failed to scratch before tippling.

The first time he drank from the newly-installed brass dish he flew in from the garden and, in midair, decided he was thirsty. Landing at a gallop he scratched to the dish and struck brass with both feet. Miniature carillon melodies sprang from its lip, filling the patio with wondrous music! Pablito continued scratching, unaware of the effect. Finally, his scratching instinct satisfied, he drank long scooping sips before leaving the dish. We could not have trained him to play such melodies. He didn't even notice. But we did and thanked him for his genius. An insane thought flashed across my mind that he might be worth keeping after all.

That night we awakened to the sound of tinkling bells. Momentarily I dreamed we drank again in the New Delhi Moghul Bar, for we were planning an Oriental trip. Comfortably seated in high-backed leather chairs, we relaxed beneath rotating fans, listening to a dozen tuned bells dangling at each chair. Heaven never seemed closer. A sari-clad maharanee glided to us carrying cooled lemon squashes and I searched for rupees when the pleasant melody jabbed me to full consciousness. Pablito's drinking dish!

Pablito, thirsty in the night (he probably had eaten an anchovy) left his bed which was strangely unusual, for he hated darkness, had found his dish and scratched. We need not have looked for we knew its origin. We arose anyway and, in the moonlight, observed Pablito scratching melodies for us. Basked in magical shadows, the moment lengthened. Then he stopped and pressed his beak into water in long, thirsty drinks. Seven times he sank into the vessel. Finally replete, he shook his head, flinging excess water from his beak, then carefully walked away and hopped back into bed, never acknowledging us at all. ➤

Chapter Twenty-One

From January until June citrus flooded Sun City. Nearly everyone owned citrus trees, but we did not. Our small garden didn't allow that privilege. We still waded in surplus because friends overwhelmed us with lemons, oranges, tangelos and grapefruit. When neighbors asked if we wanted citrus, they meant thirty grapefruit or sacks of lemons and oranges, so our garage filled with fruit waiting consumption. Seville oranges, prized and expensive elsewhere, glutted Sun City gutters and were carted to the dump at season's end after serving their stint as decorative fruit along boulevards. Utopia never was more evident in Sun City than during spring citrus season.

We froze or pasteurized everything for summer's use. Both birds enjoyed the bounty. They ate pulp and drank juice as though gulping beer on hot afternoons. When their craws filled they chased seeds around the counter. Citrus, however abundant, caused no problems. Quail devotion for tomato seeds did. It nearly caused a divorce!

Betsi and I enjoyed tomatoes as much as any fruit—maybe more—but despaired of finding tasty produce in markets. We rejected the tough-skinned, flavorless red baseballs as frauds and grew our own. Although little room existed, we somehow found space, and every year four energetic Early Girl plants snuggled against the white wall in almost obscene intimacy with bougainvillea blossoms. They flourished and bore not large, but terrifically flavorful juicy fruit sixty days after transplanting. Our stifling summer heat destroyed both blossoms and fruit so we planted in early February and counted the days until fruit ripened.

Nurtured with nitrate supplements and Arizona sunshine, the Early Girls bushed steadily and fruited hundreds of young tomatoes. We rated it a glorious sight, nearly charting the progress of each one. Pedra and Pablito also developed an interest, but only in the vines, and we did not begrudge daily snacks on bottom leaves. They soon stripped all lower foliage and even eyeballed ripening fruit but, because they sensed their established limits, they did not touch. I glowed in anticipation of the first ripe tomato. It was an annual celebration. One morning, shortly after sunrise, the quail struck first. We always blamed Pablito, but no matter. After tasting their first vine-ripened fruit, each quail commandeered all rights to the remaining harvest.

Their piratical seizure broke my heart for I had coveted that tomato. Worse, they removed only seeds, leaving the succulent mangled flesh hanging by its stem. As they ate, acidic juice squirted into their eyes and they shook their heads in quick painful spasms, then returned to seed extraction. I saw a bleak future for my tomato crop and, that morning, mounted a two-foot wire-mesh shield against their invasion.

Pablito immediately used the fence as a ladder and hopped to its top, searching into virgin branches for more ripening fruit. Pedra followed. I watched as though an invasion of killer bees had entered my kingdom and countered with double-thick black nylon netting closely pinned from ground to lattice. Fat bumblebees would have found penetration difficult and I sat in a deck chair outside, sipping iced tea revelling in my successful counterattack.

Persistent, rather than innovative, Pedra stalked the pinned border defenses. They were invulnerable. Then both birds flew investigative flights high on the net, crying for forbidden fruit barely out of reach. I nearly thumbed my nose at them. All morning they flew, scratching and pacing in fruitless missions until Betsi, in a despicable act of treachery, ran to the netting with scissors to cut an opening in my impregnable fortress when Pedra discovered the clothes-pin secret.

One by one she sharply attacked the pins (I believed her action an accident rather than a critical analysis of the problem), but the stout new pins and springs defied her beak. Yet suddenly one popped off! The impact nearly knocked her over and she staggered to her haunches, then cocked an eye jerkily at the fallen pin and slipped inside the net. Quick as she was, Pablito beat her through. Had I not seen the feat we would not have believed it. In a flurry of revenge Pedra flew to the tomatoes and destroyed four ripening fruit while

Pablito scrambled to the highest branches and filled his smaller craw. In ten minutes my tomato dream withered to a nightmare.

The sight was more than I could tolerate. I ran to the garden with new mosquito netting, intent on stopping the carnage, but Betsi stopped me. "Let them eat," she said. "God knows they've earned every seed. When you're whipped, admit it."

But I am a poor loser and after a night's meditation charged to the patch at daylight armed with additional clothes-pins, fourteen tent pegs and thirty dollars of fine mosquito netting prepared to quailproof my tomatoes even at the cost of divorce. Betsi stopped me again. "It's already as quailproof as it's going to be," she advised. "Let the children eat."

So we did. Daily they visited, bathed under bare branches, safe from hawks, and feasted on remaining foliage. Leaf by leaf and tomato by tomato their bird-like appetites demolished the entire crop. An involuntary tremor developed in my fingers, my vision thankfully blurred, but even so, I could not glance toward the garden without moaning. The patch, once handsome, trembled as a skeleton in front of the luxuriant flowering bougainvillea. "Let's tear it down," I begged. "I can't stand the sight."

"Not so soon," she demurred. "The kids are still enjoying."

She was right. No monkey bar could have given more enjoyment. They flitted from bare branch to bare branch like clumsy hummingbirds, pausing only occasionally to peck at imaginary fruit as though practicing.

Three mornings later six tomatoes miraculously appeared on the denuded vines. Like Christmas lights, small cocktail tomatoes strung across naked branches ready for pecking. The quail obliged, destroying them as enthusiastically as if they had been beefsteak fruit. Monkeys in a banana grove never had more fun.

Next morning six more tomatoes graced the vines. Although the fruit was cleverly attached with small black wires and firmly fixed, the quail pecked enthusiastically while Betsi ecstatically enjoyed the morning show. "You're salting the claim," I accused.

"What would you do?" Her eyes blended into innocence worthy of a vestal virgin. I threw up my hands.

179

And so it went. The ugly black nylon netting, like a derelict sail, covered skeletonized vines; papery bougainvillea blossoms pressed through the netting in partial camouflage and a Rufus hummingbird astonished us by building her nest in a pocket of the latticed greenery. Both quail raced eagerly each morning to the patch and wandered through the labyrinth searching, pecking and enjoying their ration of six. Envious finches, Inca doves and a cactus wren watched outside and everyone enjoyed the show. Even me.

Chapter Twenty-Two

Pablito raced through youth so fast that childhood diseases never caught up with him. He made up in other ways. In questing for an Olympic swimming team berth—quail are not natural swimmers—he grayed Betsi's hair more than all Pedra's illnesses.

Unlike hummingbirds who wildly celebrated mating rites in water-filled canna leaves and finches who skinny-dipped in frisbee orgies, our desert quail did not swim. Pablito defied tradition. One morning he lost a battle with curiosity and slipped into soapy dishwater as he monitored Betsi's dishwashing chores. While going down for the third time Betsi, at the last instant, swept him from disaster with an aluminum colander filled with knives, forks and a greasy gravy boat. While drowning he did not utter a sound as wings and eyes slowly disappeared into the soapy water. Betsi placed a small "No Swimming" sign above the sink, but I considered it worthless for Pablito seldom read notices.

We had been warned. After that we closed all bathroom doors against transient flights and emptied dishwater immediately. Thoughts of a stiffened Pablito adrift in the porcelain bowl sent us into spasms and Betsi, in a fit of prevention, even forbade leaving half-filled teacups at the breakfast table.

Pablito always assisted in our cooking and his presence was encouraged, for he added flavor to the simplest recipe. He perched on the food processor one afternoon observing Betsi mix her spiced tea blend, meditating quietly as though filing information he might use at a later time. Her special recipe of orange pekoe, lemon and orange peel, cinnamon, cloves and candied ginger mingled together fragrantly and she dumped the mixture into two large baking pans for a wedding of flavors. She turned to the oven and Pablito, who waited patiently until that second, flew with flapping wings and sharp toes into the tea mixture as if on a low level skip-bombing mission. Tea and cinnamon sticks exploded around the kitchen, atom bomb fashion, and Betsi barely turned in time to prevent a return flight. The exhilaration of success carried him swiftly through both pans to an open cupboard and, while clutching a "My Kitchen Is Clean Enough To be Healthy And Dirty Enough To Be Happy" plaque, he reconnoitered his return with eager anticipation. On hearing Betsi's sharp voice Pablito showed no remorse, but fled when she produced the vacuum. We discovered remnants of spiced tea in odd corners the next week and for more than a month, lived among odors of an Oriental spice market. We considered it excellent training for our upcoming China trip.

Another afternoon, long remembered, Pablito dug sharp toes into my scalp while appraising progress of a mango-strawberry parfait. I didn't consider it unusual that Pablito had chosen my head as an observation post in the kitchen, for all high billets attracted him. Chandeliers, overhead revolving fans and cupboard doors, at one time, had all felt his toes. Once in position, he perched like a falcon critically searching the world about him and, with his talons in my head I sensed his eyes roving about the counter. A vague uneasiness clutched my heart.

I should not have felt so. His recent excellent deportment encouraged us, and we considered tossing his dunce cap into the corner and moving him to the head of the class. He seemed, against all predicted odds, to display a certain maturity as days went by and we breathed easier.

During the previous week his voice cracked and baby cheeps vanished. Adult cries for "cup-o-tea," "cup-o-tea" filled the house, since Pablito was not a modest bird and apparently had much to say, albeit with limited vocabulary. We encouraged his growing independence and more than once he flew to the ceiling fan then, short of suicide, decided he could not fly down. On those occasions he called "cup-o-tea" loudly and repeatedly until we climbed a step ladder and carried him to the carpet. He never seemed grateful, yet we rejoiced that he had called for our help.

Now he sat, fixed to my head like a psychedelic hairpiece, while I stirred mangoes, rum and lemon juice into a bowl. His patience, surprising but welcome, caused a momentary flutter of pride for his deportment and I added gelatin and sugared egg whites to the bowl. The warm, tar-like concoction nearly filled the container and it seemed proper to reward the little bird for his interest and patience. He expected dabs of all food so I moved him, uncomplaining, to the counter and offered a small spoonful of parfait. The unusual dessert intrigued him and he pecked at it, quickly playing melodic tattoos on the spoon. The insistent rhythm aroused my curiosity and I wondered if strains of Sousa or even Dave Brubeck flowed in his veins. Certainly not Beethoven.

Only sliced strawberries remained to complete the splendid dessert. Pablito pecked happily at his prize and I turned to the refrigerator searching for berries when somehow he apparently lost interest in eating and plunged headlong, as from a diving tower, into the parfait. He sank promptly into the sugared egg whites, mango and rum quagmire. Only his beak appeared an eighth of an inch above the yellow mixture. Another split second and he would have completely disappeared. I had not seen or heard him, but sensed I had been duped and, flinging two containers of strawberries on the floor, dipped into the mess with both hands and yanked him, oozing parfait, from death.

Sticky mango dripped in reluctant ropes from his body and he remained quiet, apparently contrite, under the warm water spray. Gradually small yips burbled from his choked throat. He tested his voice several times then broke down and bawled, "Cup-o-tea," "cup-o-tea," "cup-o-tea," over and over in a mixture of adolescent accents.

He seemed like a midget under the spray. He had grown the past month, but now appeared smaller and homlier than ever and rather undesirable as a friend. He reminded me of a drowned sparrow and, shaking the squalling dwarf, I wondered why we kept him. I wanted to wring his neck!

I'll always credit Betsi's timely arrival for saving his life. She swiftly wrapped him in white cotton, blotted him dry and blew warm whispers into feathers, while cooing motherly comfort. He quieted a bit and visited as though explaining why the devil had beckoned him to active duty. The gooseneck lamp dried him quickly and for once, he appeared sober and repentant. Never had he been so clean. New feathers shone under the lamp, his small but magnificent plume puffed high and, under the heat, he looked like a featherweight champion coming out of his shower. I almost felt proud of him.

"It's nice to have another man around the house," Betsi said admiring the little curmudgeon. "He's like you in so many ways."

Suddenly, as though a bugle called, Pablito vaulted six inches into the air, his wings flapped wildly, his voice husky with excitement. "Cup-o-tea," he squawked into Betsi's face. Sheer exuberance, happiness and confidence overwhelmed him! Then prancing to table's edge, he turned with a triumphant grin, defying any possible reprimand. Despite the horrendous kitchen mess Betsi's heart melted and she grasped the quail in a frenzy of love, hugging him close to her breast. Fondly she whispered, "Please don't do that again, Pabbie. My heart won't take it."

He did not enjoy crass sentiment and wiggled from her fingers, flew to the mango bowl and, cheeping loudly, dipped his head toward the dessert. "Get away," Betsi shouted snatching him from disaster. Then turning to me she snarled, "Get rid of that stuff. This whole affair has been your fault!"

Diplomatic silence prevailed until I coaxed the parfait through the garbage disposal, not acknowledging guests might have enjoyed a feathery dessert. Betsi's sense of humor returned. "At least you could save a bit for Pabbie. He seemed to enjoy it." Indeed he did. Basking under the swing-arm lamp and cooing softly to himself, he conserved energy for other capers. In fairness he probably never planned pranks, but always seemed present when accidents occurred.

Chapter Twenty-Three

Betsi decided to wash sweaters on Sunday. "It's a perfect day," she said. She always picked perfect days by instinct, her horoscope and an invisible divining rod. After twenty years I never discovered her precise method, but it worked. My forecasts emphasized humidity, temperature and barometric pressure while she plucked hers at random. Most times she didn't even glance outside before classifying the weather. "Today," she repeated, "is a perfect day to wash sweaters." I had learned not to argue.

She did enjoy the advantage of an excellent weather forecast and an oversized thermometer registering 90 degrees by midmorning. The evaporative cooler strained atop the roof and all ceiling fans distributed cooled air throughout our home in quiet whispers. Both quail dust bathed in the herb patch early, for they did not relish intense desert heat and we faced another corker.

"Bring the trampoline to the garden," Betsi called. The broad, flat surface of the exercizing trampoline offered an ideal auxiliary drying area and we used it constantly during the summer. Long before I brought it to the patio, anxious quail cluckings floated from the garden. Sensing danger, both quail quickly left their tubs and scurried inside. I reached the patio door from the livingroom and the quail's voices raised shrilly. Unknown to me rolling trampolines fell into the same family tree with brooms and vacuum cleaners. I failed to assimilate that vital information. Even so, I nearly stopped before actually crossing the room. Thankfully they had not flown into the large revolving ceiling fan, but perched shrieking on the highest picture frame on the north wall, nearly clinging to each other in distress. Seconds later the trampoline would have been outdoors as I slowly eased it through the patio calling comforting messages.

At that moment Betsi entered from the washroom, her arms dripping with wet sweaters. Already disturbed, and unaccustomed to seeing Betsi dressed in wet sweaters, the quail mutinied. Pedra shouted an insult and arose on the gilt frame as an eagle in attack but Pablito with a thunderous crash flew headlong into the glass doors.

"Stop the carnival," Betsi shouted. "He's going to kill himself."

Her warning came too late. Pablito recovered from the floor and zoomed toward the ceiling fan. It seemed a restful haven from the trampoline. Instead, a buzz saw thumped him. The rotating blades struck as a punching bag, loosening feathers and flung him into the southwest corner facing New Mexico.

In a gesture of assistance Betsi waved wet sweaters at Pablito, but instead smacked a blinding blow alongside my face. Involuntarily I rolled the trampoline toward Pablito who flew into the fan again. The blades caught him midship and three wing feathers drifted down. He screamed loudly and dropped, wounded, to the floor, wings fluttering awkwardly. Betsi, swathed in her wet wash, scrambled on her knees desperately trying to catch the frightened bird, but he somehow managed, in a final effort, to fly, and helicoptered again into the whirling fan.

Miraculously he flew through the flack of rotating blades and dropped on the merry-go-round three inches from the ceiling. His toes firmly grasped the rotating blade, he glared down shouting threats at us and insults at the trampoline. Pedra still perched panting on the canted picture frame, aloof and terrified. Two more feathers floated to the floor and Betsi turned the fan switch off.

The blade, even at slowing speed, did not appeal to Pablito and, ill at ease, he crouched frozen until it stopped. Finally he turned to Betsi and mouthed soft pleading prayers for, surveying the trampoline still in the corner, no solution short of death appeared. He saw little hope in two swearing parents and he without a parachute. His throat vibrated wildly and deep gulps of oxygen swept through his wide open beak.

I unwound the red sweater from my face and Betsi, standing on a chair, retrieved the shuddering Pablito. "Don't move that trampoline," she commanded, "until Pabbie and Pedra are safe in the bedroom." She swept both birds into the back room and pulled all drapes.

A sense of order came over us and I rolled the trampoline to the shady sidewalk; Betsi layered the laundered Christmas cloth with sweaters then reported an all-clear signal. Lazy summer sun did its work. Hours later we discovered the quail had roosted outside on the trampoline atop their favorite cloth. Many droppings decorated it and all sweaters. After the birds bedded that night, Betsi washed again. Teenage Pablito seemed no worse for his experience but became a dedicated low altitude flyer and added ceiling fans to his list of horrors.

That night Betsi whispered into my ear. "I was wrong."

"Whadaya mean?"

"Maybe, only maybe, today wasn't a perfect day to wash sweaters."

We never closed our eyes to Pablito's trickery, for his mind worked more rapidly than ours. The devil in his heart refused to quiet and he constantly led us on merry chases. So our vigilance, always high where he was concerned, climbed to new peaks after the fan escapade. We vowed never to be caught again in the web of his caprices. How dumb we were, for Pablito saved a crowning caper the night of his sixth-week birthday. It was a natural.

We bicycled to the drugstore for new snapshots of our birds and were amazed how Pablito had grown. Nearly a young adult, he approached Pedra's girth, but better comparisons lay with a clutch of six young Gambel's quail hatched the same week on Rio Salado campus a long block away. We compared their development almost daily. Initially a slow starter, Pablito had rapidly gained weight until he appeared as large and heavy as his naturally reared cousins. Certainly he was just as active. Small rusty feathers replaced dark gray down on his head and a cocky plume carried promise of black, normal for an adult male. The white band under his chin remained obscenely clean and his voice boomed throughout the house proclaiming a macho image. Our puny baby was growing up.

Comparing him proudly with the naturally foraging family we thought of the sickly infant we knew could never survive. In fact, a promise of early death was the only reason I allowed him in the house. But Betsi claimed top honors for his survival and nothing short of disaster could have floored him now.

But the cluster of natural quail seemed healthy, too. From outward appearances they lead exemplary lives, following their parents without protest, learning basic survival skills, and maturing rapidly. The father usually perched high on a rock or bush, watching for predators while mother and chicks scratched for food. We watched proudly and considered them part of our extended family.

One warm dusky twilight we bicycled quietly to our favorite quail family habitat. Father rested on a neatly trimmed rosemary bush monitoring his family. Mother, with her hyperactive youngsters clustered around, reviewed seed gathering technics. But it was the teenagers, nearly as large as their parents, who caught our eye. Dramatic changes flashed before us in wonder! Three remained the same basic color, but almost overnight, it seemed, three developed male plumage. Changes had been rapid and flamboyant. The brilliant red caps and jet black throats so characteristic of males could not be ignored. Pablito had not yet changed so remarkably. We hurried home and examined him carefully. To our unending surprise, his white throat band had vanished and the red crown, although dusky shadows remained, no longer shone in crimson splendor. His neck, instead of black, stubbornly resisted change and indicated characteristic gray of a female. So then came the shock I would remember the rest of my days.

But Betsi spoke first. "He's a she," she said bluntly. "I haven't got a son!"

A moment or two elapsed before I found words. "We can handle that," I said thankfully ridding my mind of a family filled with half breed Pablitos. "She's Pablita instead of Pablito."

But Betsi said, "No, not even Pablita, She's not little any more. Her name is Pabla."

So Pabla she became. We accepted her curious sex change, but her disposition didn't alter a whit. She remained as irascible, flighty and independent as before. If she stayed with us she would continue to be a happy thorn in our side and when she left, God help her mate!

So Pabla deceived us to the end. The only way she would have surprised us more would have been to drop an egg in our lap. We suspected she had that in mind. Yet we did not fault her strongly, for deception lay in our laps too. We had not told the girls about our China trip! 🦃

Chapter Twenty-Four

We need not have told them. They knew. How they knew! Next Sunday we test-packed luggage and the quail instantly smothered us with suspicion. I had not meant to alert Pedra, but I did. With puzzled mistrust she shadowed me to the bathroom and leaped—an action never taken before—deep inside the sink cabinet as I dropped to my knees searching for extra toothpaste. She balanced, on one leg, her bright eyes examining every move. Small quail sounds echoed within the cabinet clearly questioning my unusual behavior.

Pabla crow-hopped to our open bags and stalked across packed clothing. Even in immaturity she presented every sign of a nesting urge. Scratching and cooing, she quickly shaped T-shirts and socks into a bowl and fluffed comfortably inside the phony nest, watching and waiting, like a bird with a definite purpose in life. She appeared settled for the duration, whatever that was.

Returning to the bedroom Pedra flew to the bed, bored into our open luggage and hid, under a melange of sweaters and socks, her restless head twitching this way and that within the tumbled underclothing. Their hyperexcitability disturbed us and would have been insufferable were they not so pathetic.

But how did they know? Long ago we questioned quail intelligence, but at times, they stomped those doubts into oblivion seeming far smarter than we. Other times the Cro-Magnon man rated a Rhodes scholarship compared to Gambel's quail. If Betsi tapped a plastic mealworm cup both quail, when hungry, double-timed to her as if magnetized. Pedra waited for me at nap time and always pulled her curtain at night. When darkness descended in the garden and the quail still bathed or hunted we often called them inside. Without hesitation, at the sound of our voice, they stopped whatever their chore and pranced unerringly through the two-inch opening. Never did they fly into glass windows as other birds did. Why?

But the bathroom's location was another matter! Pedra never learned it. Long desperate cries called to me during my first bath after camping, for she thought herself deserted. Betsi brought her to me and she perched happily at the tub's rim watching my strange latherings. The next day, when I was deep in suds, Pedra wailed from the next room. Betsi laughed and carried her to me again. She perched contentedly on the rim and visited while I scrubbed, preening a hundred or so feathers that escaped her previous attention.

Two hundred baths later, if I did not carry her with me—and I usually did—she wailed continuously from other rooms as though I had plunged into the River Styx, even though she clearly heard my splashing. After searching several rooms she might stumble into the bathroom, her sobs ceasing on sighting me, and fly to the tub as though she had made a magnificent discovery. Then, more often than not, she leaped across the watery moat and pecked hair on my chest or preened her own feathers. Why? Quail behavior was part of the puzzle.

We wondered why they fussed while we packed for China. Intelligence? Instinct? Premonition? We didn't know. We did know their gizzards tumbled in a frenzy over our preparation and under no circumstances was their behavior to be classified flapdoodle. They were serious!

China travel for Gambel's quail was impossible. Even Betsi admitted that. Yet the birds had been such an intimate part of our lives their demand for inclusion was reasonable. Even China. Now we were leaving and they felt...cheated.

Our Phoenix daughter promised to care for the birds in her sunny oleander-fringed home. The birds would neighbor with parakeets in an already screened porch and we intended taking beds, corduroy, drinking dishes and garlic so departure would not be overly traumatic. In the end predeparture shock claimed all four of us.

Packing continued and the bird's excitement increased. They possessively settled on packed clothing then scrambled to our shoulders and chattered protests at us. Betsi matched their intensity. With both pleading birds watching, she studied the comfortable bedroom, her eyes computerized the firm-mattressed bed, children's pictures in younger days, an unfinished afghan and tears came easily. "This trip's a ghastly mistake. We can't leave our quail." She started unpacking.

A sharp pain of indigestion stabbed my stomach. Her declaration was no shock. Symptoms had been building and the explosion simply exposed her festering hurt. Yet I was unprepared. We stood silently facing each other for a moment, both aware of her enormous decision. Words slowly came. "You'd rather stay with...these...birds...instead of going to China?"

Betsi did not hesitate. Hours of wretched dreams had drained her face and darkness settled around her voice. "Let me remind you that these little quail are the most wonderful thing that's happened to me since retirement...and that includes China or any other place."

The dangerous glint in her eye fascinated me and quick reasoning shouted the necessity for delicate diplomacy. "For God's sake be quiet and agree with everything she says," I told myself. "It's the only chance for success." I kissed her on the cheek (always safe) and touched both birds lightly on their plumes. Pedra moved to my side while Pabla nimbly hopped into a bed of handkerchiefs and buried herself. "You're absolutely right," I emphasized after waiting a moment as though meditating. "This trip is a mistake."

Both quail stopped chattering. Betsi's eyes widened and tears slowed. She dabbed them with an unpacked washcloth and whistled in surprise. "You honestly mean that?"

In moments of necessity I lie easily. This was one of those moments. "Absolutely. I've had doubts, too. I don't think our children could manage the birds." I kissed her forehead and placed both arms around her.

Pedra and Pabla disappeared at the sound of her whistle but, sensing deception, drifted to Betsi's ear and mumbled quietly. Then Betsi said, "Our daughter could care for them easily, and she wants them. It's just that...I'd miss them and they'd miss me, too." Both quail nodded sideways at me and trotted along her shoulder. It was three against one.

With my back pressed against diplomatic ropes and no room to maneuver, I had to compromise or throw in the towel. "I'll cancel the trip," I said recklessly, then clamped my jaws tightly closed, thunderstruck that I had uttered such a ridiculous statement and wondering what idiotic statement I might utter next.

Both quail stopped prancing on Betsi's shoulder and her mouth flew open. "Good," she shouted in relief, the sunny

191

side of her disposition reappearing. "I never wanted to see the Great Wall."

I got busy thinking and, not making much progress, heard myself say, "We can get a partial refund from the airline, but the China tour will be a total loss."

"Total?" She shuddered as though an electric shock had violated her toenails and I cast my eyes skyward thanking Him for Betsi's Scottish ancestors.

"Total," I lied emphatically, for we carried cancellation insurance. "No refund now. Someone is heating tea for us in China at this moment." And because the word had such a friendly ring I repeated, "Total!"

Betsi's eyes battled the depressing information. Pedra and Pabla murmured anxiously on her shoulder, their prancing slowed to a walk. A few tears still dripped down her cheek, "It isn't China alone. When you start travelling you never want to come home." She suspiciously kicked the pile of maps at my feet.

I could not deny her accusation. "I'm older now," I said defensively.

She snorted and the birds shuddered. "You were older then. You never want to come home," she continued, recalling a supposedly brief retirement Mexican fling that extended to seven months; another time we stretched a Caribbean reconnaissance into a year's South Seas experience and now a month's trip to China and Mongolia faced her. Betsi's excellent memory wounded me so I hit her in the pocketbook again.

"Forget the money. Let's scrub the entire trip," I said.

She bit her lip. "We can't do that. We have too much invested."

I noted her hesitation and perceived it to be a lucky omen. "Whatever you say. It's your decision, Bets."

"We can't waste our investment. We'd better go."

My heart leaped. "You really want to go to China?"

"Yes, yes, yes! Let's go," she shouted above quail protests.

"Only if you insist," I said and silently raised the victory flag.

She made a serious study of my face and found innocence staring at her. "Home after China? No side trips?" she asked. I nodded.

So, with the gift of Pedra's coos in our ears (Pabla unexpectedly remained silent) and promises to return in a month, we repacked and fled to the Phoenix airport next day.

We climbed the Great Wall on a blustery cold autumn day and marvelled at the terra-cotta warriors in Xian. Inner Mongolian hosts spread blankets in a yurt for us and we viewed Mao's body in Beijing. Drifting along the Grand Canal toward Shanghai, our whirlwind month vanished and, leaving the tour, we flew to Hong Kong alone.

An anxious call home assured us both quail were happy, healthy and apparently did not miss us, so I plotted a course to Thailand, Burma and Nepal, throwing in Kashmir and India for good measure. Three and a half months later in Hong Kong we called home again and received assurances our quail still lived and apparently did not recognize our absence.

Betsi was appalled. "We've been gone the equivalent of nine years in a quail's life," she calculated. "They've forgotten us." I quickly confirmed homeward flights for our travel fund was depressingly low.

Bird memory has long been questioned. Instinct yes, memory a question mark. We did not know. We thought they remembered certain individuals—favorably or otherwise—but were never certain. On the other hand, they might run halfway to a broccoli tidbit, stop, and their thought train broken, never reach the food. Now we speculated again regarding bird memory. Would they remember us?

The enormity of our defection weighed heavily as we flew home. Pedra would be middle age, half her life gone. Pabla would be full grown, past teen age. Both would have dramatically changed. What would their response to us be? And, God help us, maybe they had died! (Our daughter wouldn't dare tell us on the telephone!) We never mouthed those thoughts during the long flight and the wonder of our Oriental adventure faded as we flew to Los Angeles. I secretly agreed with Betsi: the trip had been a ghastly mistake if we had lost our two friends.

As soon as our daughter's house appeared my heart stopped. I wanted to turn back, but no escape existed. Strange constrictions bottled my breath, my throat tightened and my heart stumbled and throbbed in a series of excited hiccups. I gripped the wheel tighter to keep from trembling.

Uncontrollably my eyes watered and I felt ashamed to wipe them.

Betsi sat beside me as calm as if going to a basket social, but the fear of happiness clawed at my throat and threatened to choke me as we neared the small white house. My fists clenched the steering wheel fiercely and I found it almost impossible to unclasp them as we arrived. "This is dumb," I told myself. "Dumb!" Somehow the car stopped.

"We're here," Betsi said brightly. "Let's see our family." She thrust a peace offering of fresh broccoli into my hand.

Numbly I left the car and stumbled toward the house. I wanted to race madly up the walk, throw open the door and shout hellos, but discipline overcame me and I conversed cheerfully with Betsi as we strolled along. Betsi later said I never uttered a word.

The door opened and we were inside. Kisses, bone-breaking handshakes and thank-God-you're homes flowed and finally the birds came into focus. I hardly knew them. Both preened calmly on the couch as sunlight bathed their bodies. One, much larger and more beautiful, pecked a wing feather; the other considerably smaller, reached into the oil gland and dipped her head between her legs to oil breast feathers. A definite deforming depression creased her left side. Pedra.

We stepped toward them and both continued preening. I called, but my voice failed. "Peddie, Pabbie, we're home!" Betsi shouted.

Pedra glanced up and examined us without interest. She spoke several times to herself, her head bobbed indecisively, then slowly stopped. Recognition started in her eyes, a joyous cry escaped her throat, and the heavy weight of love chained her earthbound for a millisecond, then she exploded from the couch as though exorcizing a thousand demons. Fluttering wings stormed at my head and Pedra landed in my hair, puffing as though she had crossed the Atlantic. Her open mouth panted for oxygen and when she gained her breath, she hopped to my shoulder and chattered excitedly, her garlic breath unmistakable. Underlying the hysterical chatter a subtler statement surfaced: "Oh, I'm glad you're back. Don't ever leave me again."

Pabla, atop Betsi's arm gazed at her in wonderment and jabbered the same message. "Don't ever leave us!"

We never did. ➤

Afterward

Last year soon after the oranges bloomed and carob pods vanished from the sidewalk, a brazen, lusty male Gambel's quail fluttered into the open patio. His noisy entrance among chairs and houseplants was not unnoticed and Pedra and Pabla flew to my lap. A week later when dusk settled around the marigolds and Pabla feasted on green cabbage worms in the garden, the male called again. Unknown to us, she answered. They eloped that night.

Next evening she fluttered her wings defiantly at us from the garden wall, shrieked a single freedom call, then ignored us forever. We see her almost nightly, for she brings her family of six for rations—Betsi provides ample food for the entire quail community—but does not acknowledge us in any way. Her mate seems an amiable sort and, since she is happy, so are we.

Pedra is old and arthritic. At the moment she is obsessed with the nesting urge and confidently sits on three sterile eggs and an empty black 35mm film cartridge. She peers at us myopically from a kitchen-drawer nest, half hidden amidst a warm collection of facial tissue, only emerging briefly for a drink and sparse rations. She never seems hungry. In a week or two she will toss in the towel and come to us, barely able to walk, her feathers dropping in great puffs and looking like a worn old bag lady. Gradually new feathers will sprout and she will limp about the house, flying nightly to her beloved bed on the kitchen bookshelf. Sometimes we must help her. There she will rest, looking down at us with solemn black eyes, never once realizing what a joy she has been to our retirement years.

Order Form

Send to:
Quantum Press of Arizona
17823 99th Drive
Sun City, AZ 85373

Name _____

Street _____

City _____

State _____Zip _____

Send $6.95 for each book ordered. Shipping: Add $2.00 for the first book and $1.00 for each additional book. Arizona residents add .30 tax per book.

Number of books _____x $6.95   _____

Shipping   _____

Arizona sales tax (AZ residents only)   _____

Amount Enclosed   _____

Make checks payable to **Quantum Press of AZ**.